MORE PR

MW01698207

Petals of Grace

Essential Teachings for Self-Mastery

"Reading *Petals of Grace* is like having all the layers of egoic self, thought, and anxieties dissolve in the brilliance, clarity and love that emanates from the word of Sai Maa. She says, "The next evolutionary step is to realize that you are divine." Step-by-step she reveals to us the Divinity we are, takes our hand in hers and as a loving sister pours feminine Shakti into our being so that we can command the blueprint of our full potential self to take dominion within ourselves, now. A feminine all-inclusive master for the 21st century has arrived."

Barbara Marx Hubbard, President, Foundation for Conscious Evolution. Author of *Emergence: The Shift from Ego to Essence; Conscious Evolution: Awakening the Power of Our Social Potential; The Revelation: A Message of Hope for the New Millennium*

"Sai Maa brings the reader into the sphere of Divine love. When you bask in the glow of her book you receive the Darshan of her presence."

Rabbi Zalman Schachter-Shalomi, author of *Wrapped in a Holy Flame: Teachings and Tales of the Hasidic Masters*

"Sai Maa knows the heart of the feminine, speaks woman to woman, and offers every human being the path to our divine essence. I trembled as I read this book that revealed Sai Maa knows me better than I know myself."

Rabbi Malka Drucker, author of *White Fire: A Portrait of Women Spiritual Leaders in America*

"There are those among us whose profound spiritual essence cheers the soul and brings peace and joy to the heart. Sai Maa is one of those whose unconditional love ignites our own spiritual identity and helps deepen our chosen service to humanity during these challenging times.

In savoring her beautiful writings of truth and encouragement, I recommend allowing her energies to touch your life as they have selflessly enriched mine and empowered so many others."

Virginia Essene, international speaker and author/co-author of 9 metaphysical books including *Energy Blessings From the Stars* and *New Teachings for an Awakening Humanity*

"This book is a welcomed treat of enlightenment for the body, mind and spirit. It crosses the boundaries of all religions and gives insight to our collective humanity in unity. Sai Maa's words bring us mysteriously face to face with Truth, Love, and Light that is in the Divine within and without. A must read book for your own self-realization."

Reverend Dr. Thomas L. Brown, pastor and professor, Ebenezer Missionary Baptist Church and Martin University

"While reading this book with an open heart, the energy of love, power, peace and joy flow in. The teachings of Sai Maa are for feeling with the heart more than thinking with the mind, for her words carry the light of her love."

Dr. Judith S. Moore, physician and author, *Healing from the Heart: the Inherent Power to Heal from Within*

Petals of Grace

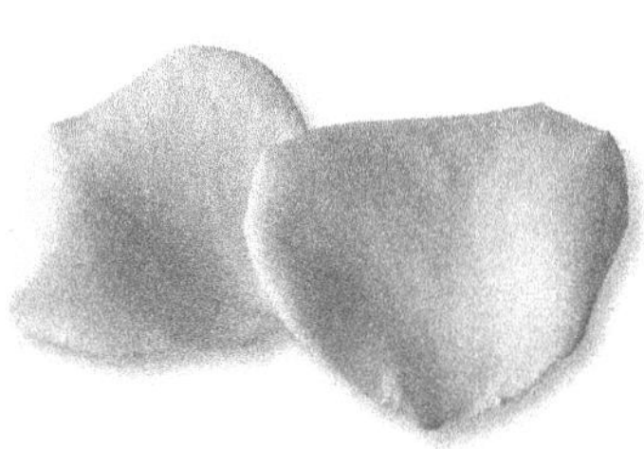

Petals of Grace

Essential Teachings for Self-Mastery

Sai Maa

Petals of Grace
Essential Teachings for Self-Mastery, 2nd Edition

Printed in the United States of America
1st Printing, June 2005
2nd Printing, July 2007
3rd Printing, September 2012
4th Printing, January 2014

ISBN: 978-0-9885197-4-9
Library of Congress Control Number: 2005924852

Sai Maa

Sai Maa, LLC
303-996-0123
www.sai-maa.com

Contents

Foreword

By Marianne Williamson

The first time I met Sai Maa, she was standing in my driveway in the middle of the day. She was a petite woman wearing a large white hat, holding a bouquet of flowers, and looking at me quizzically, as though sizing up my life.

Inside the house, we exchanged pleasantries before she offered to speak to me privately. We went into another room, I lay down on a couch, and she spoke to me of things about myself that I didn't think another human being could possibly know. She seemed to be reading an x-ray of my soul, understanding what was ruptured and hurt inside me, and knowing what to do about it.

At the time, I was suffering through a dark and painful episode in my life, and felt deeply depressed. The week before I met Sai Maa, I remember crying out from my bed in the middle of the night, "God help me." And I believe He did, in part through that petite woman who was standing in my driveway holding flowers in the sun.

While I can't remember what Sai Maa said to me at my house that day, I know that by the time I sat up, I was convinced I was in the presence of a woman with profound and even holy insight. I have experienced her ability to bring down a light from some holy realm and fill darkened places in my mind and heart.

When my life force was so battered that doctors were warning of the onset of disease, I could feel hopelessness impressing itself upon every aspect of my being. Sai Maa called me back from the edge. I don't know how else to put it. I feel as if she saved my life. I don't know the processes by which a woman could receive the kind of power she has, but Sai Maa knows things about the journey of my soul that only someone very close to the Mind of God could know.

And even more than that, when she has promised to help me with this or that pain in my heart, she has. I have felt her pour a spiritual medicine into my veins, and I consider it one of the greatest blessings of my life that I have met her. My hope is that whoever reads this book gets a dose of Sai Maa's medicine. I know what that medicine has done for me, and I wish it for you.

May we all be healed.

From the Heart of a Child

During a visit to the Indiana Women's Prison, the following letter was written and given to Sai Maa by a child attending the summer day camp held for incarcerated mothers and their children.

The words that Sai Maa said made a warm feeling inside, like when she said, "I love you." It didn't feel weird, it felt right. It felt like she knew me. It's like when she talked to me, it felt like Jesus was talking to me. And when she looked in my eyes, I felt like I was a baby being held! She looked in my eyes and it felt like she was reading me.

When she hugged me, she said, "You will do great things." When she touched my arms, it was like she gave me a vibe of "Don't worry, you'll be fine!"

When she was talking, it was feeling like my heart was writing the words she said in me. I could feel her words writing on my body. It was so peaceful and felt like she knew me my whole entire life, but I just met her!

I still feel her touching me. Her smell, her perfume was just amazing. It was the freshest smell. It was like God's breath.

Sai Maa offers aarti to her guru, Sri Sathya Sai Baba.

Dedication

To Sri Sathya Sai Baba

My Baba,

In all I am, at your feet
In all I am, in the center of your shining
Golden bright Light . . . your heart
In all I am, watching you unfold
Each of us with Glory,
With the Grace of your divine Love.

In eternity,
Your ever,

Sai Maa

Sai Maa in Japan offering her loving support to those affected by the devastating natural disasters in 2011.

1

Be the Embodiment of Love

Allow your Self to be transformed by Love.

Let the music of Love melt your heart.

Let Divinity fill your heart with Love.

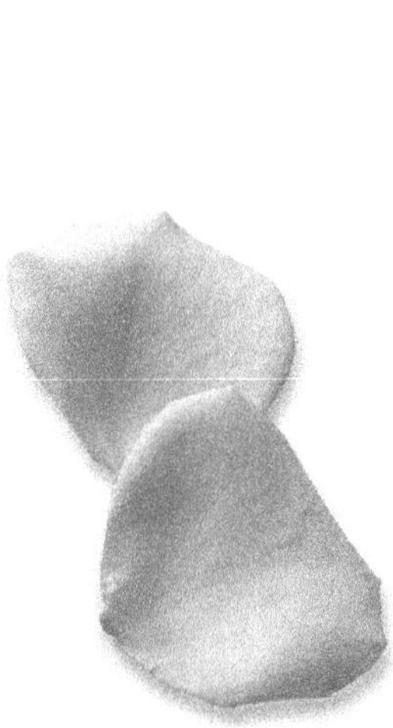

Be the Embodiment of Love

Love Is the Highest Truth

Beloveds, know that when you yearn for the Light, you get it. How many of you focus, center yourself, and think of the Light? Your attention most of the time goes to other matters. The highest priority, however, is for you to experience the Higher Self.

The Light or Paramatma (the Supreme Self, the Absolute) is devotion, this selfless Love, pure Love for the Creator. Always remember, Love is the highest truth. Love is truth, and every single thing comes from Love. Through Love, freedom is experienced. Of course, I'm not just speaking of your Love for your offspring or partner. There is no virtue greater than Love. The universe comes from Love, the universe is sustained by Love, and the universe merges in Love. When you are devoted to this pure, divine, selfless Love in a practical way, you will be enlivened and aware that you are sustained by Love. You will live in it, eat in it, sleep in it, and work in it. The more you feel sustained by this devotional Love, the more you will yearn for it. Ultimately you will merge with this divine Love.

This power of Love will unveil the illusion of the worldly life and take you beyond the world of physicality to the world of supreme bliss, which has no birth and no death. This Love permeates the whole world, the whole universe. How many of you are aware of this power? An experience of life without faith and without Love is full of separateness, and thus, full of pain.

This devotion, this selfless Love or Godly Love, can achieve everything. With a devoted heart you will always receive divine Grace—divine Grace together with devotion. You will experience cosmic Love embraced in bliss, another aspect of pure Love. When I say Love is God, God is Love, I mean Love is a *form* of God. All forms are God in essence. How aware are you of this sacred Love? How do you use this Love? Know this power is right here for you, and if you choose to live in faith, this Love will be present and you will experience peace. When you experience peace, you will feel truth.

So be devoted. Give more Love, give *more*. Pour Love into every atom and be the embodiment of Love itself. Transmute so-called negative or dark emotions—doubt, anger, envy, greed, jealousy—if you choose, by embracing them with your Love, so pure, so bright, and so magnificent. This Love is in you. Go inward, because the outer world will never give this to you. You are then a "real" human being. Play with the Creator. The inner world is a playground and the Creator is waiting for you with Love.

Now ask yourself if Love is the undercurrent of all your actions. Self-inquiry is needed if you feel no satisfaction in your heart. When there is no feeling of Love in your prayers or meditation practice or when your japa (mantra repetition) is dry,[1] it's better to stop because the practice is not serving you. Still, yearn for this Love, and you can experience the beauty, the innocence, and the sweetness of this experience of life that you have been given.

When you emanate Love, you can walk into a room, and the hearts of all those in the room will melt. You do not have to do anything. When a heart melts and opens, the Shakti (spiritual energy) and Grace do their work, and then your every moment becomes effortless.[2]

Therefore, let everything, let all, merge with that precious, unique, Godly Love. That Love will always uplift you and take you to joy, the joyous heart of a young child living fully in the "now." Once you choose to live in that Love, deep transformations will occur.

How many of you are ready to develop this unique Love within? You may say, "I'm ready, Sai Maa, I'm ready," but I see a great deal of doubt, so be sincere with yourself. Are you ready, or is there still some fear? When you say, "I'm ready," you must be ready, without fear and doubt, to be one with the infinite, the devotion, to be one with purity and sincerity.

Please, embrace all within you. Be ready and you will receive all. Some of you ask, "Will I see God one day?" To receive the vision, much Love is needed. God is right here in front of you, but because your eyes are veiled you cannot see. Divine Grace will grant you the vision, depending on your devotion.

Beloved, fill your mind with the fragrance of pure devotional Love, and then your mind can *emanate* this purity of Love. Again, what effort are you making to *live* in this Love? Allow your Self (or consciousness) to be transformed by Love. Let the music of Love melt your heart. Let Divinity fill your heart with Love.

A devoted one asked, "What does Sai Maa want?" Sai Maa wants you to be resolved to live in Love and to embrace all your qualities with Love and to love all.

Love Transforms All Attachments

All of you must practice Love. All want to be loved, and this Love is Divinity. The miracle of the life principle originated from Divinity, and it is bound to merge in Divinity. When you remember that the principle of Self is the same in everyone, then you will be humble.

Live in that humble, pure mind and move away from attachments. Love transforms all attachments. Allow the principle of Love to transmute all impurities, and realize humanity is *sacred humanity*. Then experience divine union and merge in and with God. The Light of Love can never be extinguished.

2

The Grace Latent in All

This God, this Source,

Oneness, Creation resides inside of you

and can be experienced in a second.

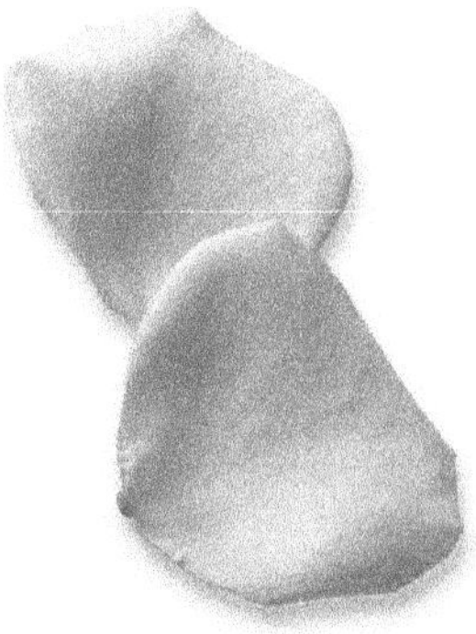

The Grace Latent in All

Recognize Your Divine Light

The power of Grace, the Grace latent in all, is in absolutely all things. When this Grace is awakened, activated, and nurtured, it keeps on flowing gracefully, and you will experience the magnificence of life. This Grace takes you to truth.

Until you experience truth, the mind will play tricks, and the personality will fall into despair, trusting the ego and the mind, which are not yet purified. You will have no peace. Sometimes because of "happiness" you will think, "Oh, this is it." No, this is the surface. You are "happy," which is the surface, for a reason. I can see there is no peace, because real peace is experienced in even the chaotic moments. When you lose your job, your parents die, the house burns, your partner, wife or husband drops you, your kids leave, there's no more money, or your business is over—when your world is collapsing—*then* are you at peace? Are you surrendering? Are you living in fear or living in faith and peace?

No peace is possible if there is struggle, tightness, fear, and war within yourself. So how can there be peace on this plane if there is war within you? Peace is about each of us. Some are even saying this world is becoming hell. Well, who is creating the hell? The inhabitants of this earth. "All ways" remember, heaven or hell, good or bad, right or wrong are within the minds of humans themselves. What is your *choice*?

When your intellect is purified, when your mind accepts awareness, then through training it is easier to grasp even for one minute the law of consciousness, the Supreme Intelligence, and the Supreme Power called God or Source or Creator. What do you understand by the word "God"? How do you see God? The way God *is* or the way you *want* to see God? Do you choose or wish to see God or do you say, "I'll put my attention on that at another time"? And you look for a job, for money, a partner or whatever. For most, attention to the soul is left until the last moment or for tomorrow, which does not exist. Again, you can see that with free will, with your hand, *you* create your own world, your own healing, your own heaven, or the life experience you choose.

This God, this Source, Oneness, Creation resides *inside* of you and can be experienced in a second. This is an immense power that is beyond mind or emotions, and each of you carries it. When you give attention to it, you live above all worldly maya (ignorance or illusion). You then see that this world is free in itself. Baba says, "Change your glasses from fear to Love, and you will see this world in its real beauty."

You who have meditated for a long time and are not fully getting the "juice" of your practice, I ask you to allow some doors to open in your being. I invite you to be a beginner, to drop the pride of all the courses you have taken or all the gurus or spiritual teachers you have met or all the mantras you have received. Be humble. Be new. This moment of renewal is full of the miracle of Creation itself. This is the law of life—constant change, constant evolution. Drop all your *ideas* about enlightenment and drop all expectations that the mind has created based on non-truth.

Live for your soul and live for your purpose with no fear. The purpose of a human life is to seek and discover the Great Self residing within, that God we all think or talk about. Every moment carries this possibility, but because of your feeling of separation, this Presence is not experienced and most of you live in duality, swinging from fear to Love, from Love to fear. This fear is so powerful that it shakes you. Your thought patterns bathe in that fear to such an extent that you are afraid of your own feelings, your own power, trusting fear more than anything else, even placing faith in these feelings of fear.

Of course, you wish to "all ways" be happy. Every person wishes to be happy. Whatever you do is for the sake of happiness, *but* it never lasts because it is always coming from a reason outside of you. Have you noticed how you seek happiness in every single action? It is simply because your essence is joy—divine joy resides within you—and feelings of grandeur will reveal and awaken this inner joy. This inner joy needs always to be remembered.

The joy that you experience in the outer world, however, is nothing but a tiny spark compared to your own inner joy. Use the mind as a worker and go inside yourself. There you will find the amrit (elixir of life) of the joy you are seeking. The outside world will never give you this satisfaction because you are looking for *divine* joy, which you receive only when you are in contact with the divine truth within.

Naturally, when you stop identifying with the mind, you will feel your own Divinity. Living in your body is the I AM (the Godself, your I AM Presence), and this I AM is above and beyond all things created in the world.[1] This I AM is Absolute, is pure divine consciousness within you, and this consciousness lives to be loved by you. This Love is found only in your own heart, not in any reading, because most reading material is created from and of the mind. Only then will the personality or mind experience bliss. You *know* you have the freedom to choose.

Stillness will give you that divine consciousness. Be still. Know I AM God. Stillness will allow you to master your senses, the I AM Absolute or consciousness will take over, and purity will come to the surface. Only then, eternity *is*. If you function with the mind that "all ways" wanders around, there will always be pain. Only your true Divinity, this I AM, will remove that pain and give peace.

Meditation is beyond that pain or pleasure. Still, do not be proud of any meditation experience. It is a watching state, a witness state, a state of Self, of God. The mind will give you ideas. You also know these ideas will change, so how can you trust the mind? Meditation allows your inner you, the Invisible, to unfold. After it unfolds, you can be in *any* action, and it will still be unfolded. Then, much pure divine energy will pour itself into your whole being, and from that consciousness everything can be and is created.

Such freedom is experienced because this consciousness is freedom itself. This consciousness is pure energy and with it you can create anything. This consciousness is so free it cannot be "stained." This consciousness lives in your breath, and this very breath takes you to its Creator, directly.

Because of your lack of awareness, you may not recognize this consciousness or see the brightness of your own Light. And there is "no thing" to attain—there is only to feel, perceive, accept, be aware of, and be in contact with. This is possible through feelings of Love, because the mind carries too many filters to permit the direct experience unless you spend years purifying it. This Light is you and every instant *is*—is shining brightly in your heart. When you connect with true feelings (meaning non-fear based feelings), you experience the Presence of this glorious Light. This is you!

3

The Source of Joy and Bliss

You are to go inward to experience your inner joy first. Real joy never, ever ends—it is transcendent, it is full.

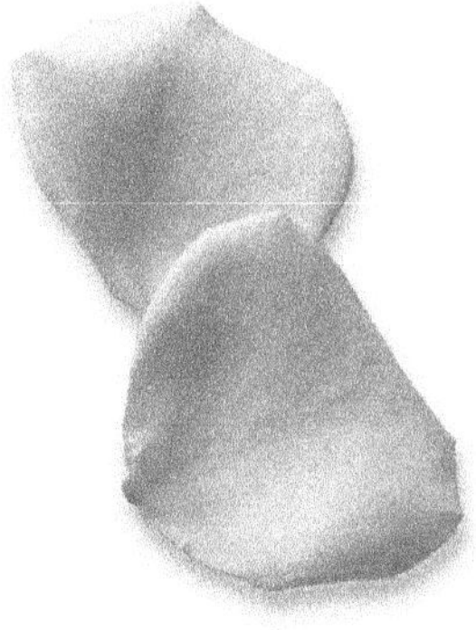

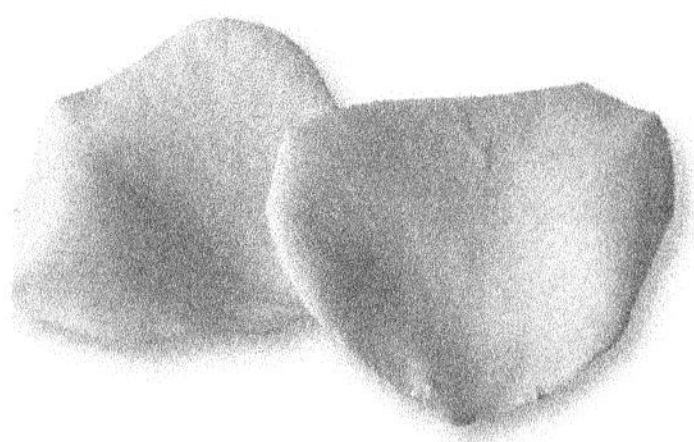

The Source of Joy and Bliss

Happiness Comes from Reason—Joy Comes from Inside

True, real happiness cannot, *cannot* be found in things that change and pass away, such as *relationships, marriage*, and so forth. Whatever comes and goes will definitely bring pain as well as happiness. You may or may not be happy. You may get married (I am not yet convinced that marriage brings great joy). I cannot say you will be happy, even though I hear that you want happiness. Look within and you will find the joy of the Self. Then you will know what "real" is. Happiness is from reason, whereas joy comes from inside.

The ideas of "pain," "pleasure," "hard," "difficult," and "easy" are all in the mind and these ideas change constantly. You cannot rely on a single idea of your mind, because it's all in a state of distress. Know that pain is the *background* of pleasure, as none of these worldly things last. They come and go.

So if you say you are confused, know that *you* are not confused, as you are the Self. The *mind* is confused. Of course the mind is confused! Use introspection and ask yourself, "What brings confusion?" Be alert. Be aware.

Do not be a slave to your wants or desires. Do you think a husband, children, a house, a car, a job, or a family will give you the joy that you are longing for? Please stop wanting. It is a vicious circle. Detach yourself from all that makes your mind restless. *"No thing" among these is permanent. Nothing.*

Only the changeless is permanent. Whatever changes cannot be permanent! Of course you want permanent happiness, permanent joy, but you do not know what "permanent" is. Permanence means unfailing memory throughout time. Eternalize your consciousness, your memory, in the infinite vibration of time. Permanency, like true joy, is that which does not change, unlike the mind which changes constantly.

The Eternal Power of Joy

The Creator creates all of us in His or Her own image with joy, out of joy, and full of joy; thus, it is your heritage—it is your birthright—to be joyous all the time. It is easier actually to be joyous than to be depressed, because joy is your essence. No one can take real, true joy away from you; no one can steal your inner joy.

Joy is very different from happiness. There is a reason for happiness, whereas joy comes from the Source of pure Love. Real joy is easily spread and transforms you instantly. Inner joy is formless and beyond the happiness provided by the senses—it is the source of all Source and can only exist when you go inward, because this joy comes from your Supreme Self.

You will become intoxicated with this joy, dancing in ecstasy, not even knowing that dancing is going on, so intoxicating is the Love of joy, the joy of Love. Outer joy is a limited expression of divine, inner joy. Your Presence is joy; the cool air brings joy; sitting together is joy; the blessing of the sun is joy.

All of Creation is full of joy, pregnant of and with joy—the entire universe bestows the Grace of joy.

Joy is pulsating in your cells, creating a loving feeling in you. This loving feeling takes you to peace. Because your true spirit is joy, nothing can disturb it when it arises from within. This bliss is the true nature of your own inner God.

How blessed, then, are we to be the embodiments of joy, the joy of a flower, the gentleness of joy from our eyes, tears of joy from our hearts, the unique, splendid joy of serving. The Divine grants joy. How precious is joy, which carries so much power that as it unfolds its petals, the sound resonates and echoes in the universe.

So welcome joy, My Beloveds, welcome joy.[1] It is the Atma (the Self, the Higher Self), and there is no room for doubt when you are in this state of bliss. Taste it, drink it, feel it around your being, share it with all, and transmit this joy to everyone you meet. This is your dharma (right action), to express joy in the universe.

For lunch I was given papaya to eat, and the pieces of fruit were saturated with Love, with joy. It was such a joy to eat these pieces of fruit offered by God and prepared by God. We are blessed. We are so loved that even the fruit expresses its Love in our physical being.

This is how precious it is to experience the joy of the universe. You are to go *inward* to experience your inner joy first. Real joy never, ever ends—it is transcendent, it is full. Merge your awareness with the joy of the universe. Joy and contentment are divine qualities within each of you, and when you live in bliss, you taste the amrit of God's Love. It's so easy to allow bliss to fill your being, because it's your own essence. Infuse yourself with the grandeur of joy, the purity of joy. It will definitely take you to the kingdom of Mother-Father Creator, because true joy is exceedingly powerful. It comes directly from the Source; and to be one with the Source, you have to move beyond "good," "bad," "right," and "wrong," beyond duality to where there is no more disappointment.

This joy is also full of compassion and leads you to truth, to the Self, leads you to God. The One is the embodiment of joy, is Spirit, and those who practice sadhana (spiritual practice) know inner joy. Devotion leads you to divine joy, a joy that none can take away. In the secret of your greatness, deep, deep joy is waiting to express itself, to reveal itself to you.

I was in awe while one of you described the great flood of bliss in your being, waves of bliss, nothing but bliss. Bliss is your essence, the essence of your cells, these waves of joy I see when you come to me, joy mixed with innocence, so joyous, so delightful, so precious. All of you are to be aware of this bliss, this Godly joy, this joy of togetherness.

4

The Truth of Relationships

If you choose to move into a relationship where it's only glory,
only victory, only Oneness, only Unity, and Divinity,
then the sharing will be so magnificent and
so powerful that the breath that you both breathe
will merge with the whole universe.

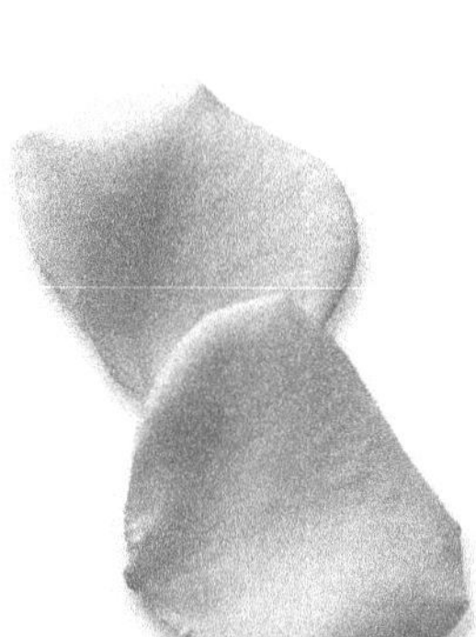

The Truth of Relationships

The Limitations of Fear and Need

Most of the time you move into a relationship because you are lonely, or perhaps you are afraid of being by yourself. Also, sometimes out of depression, boredom, or physical need, you choose a relationship. How is it possible for a relationship to be harmonious if these are the main reasons the relationship exists?

Many of you carry the fear of your old relationship into your new relationship. By this I mean that many of you have come out of a relationship because your partner has found another, and you have been hurt and you are angry. When your next relationship comes, you feel, "I hope he doesn't leave me" or "I hope she doesn't leave me. Oh my God, I don't want to suffer like last time." You're bringing the past into the "now" moment, then you cannot be in the "now" anymore. You cannot be fresh in this new relationship. In every relationship where there is fear, know that you are not free.

Do you understand this? Do *not* move into a relationship with these old patterns. When you start wishing for a relationship, ask yourself, "For what reason am I longing or looking for a relationship?" There are many purposes for a relationship, *many* purposes. Ask yourself, "Am I moving into this relationship for a purpose? If so, what is the purpose of this relationship?"

You need to realize that each relationship is sacred, each relationship is new, each is divine and unique. And you need to remember to share in your relationship. You may think that you don't have any needs, but *think* about this. Look carefully. Within each of you, on each side of the relationship, there is an emptiness that is longing, searching to be filled. And that's not the truth of a relationship. You say to another person, "I love you," but what are you really saying? What conditions are you placing on this relationship? What are your expectations? Is this relationship fresh? Is it spontaneous? Are you canceling all the freedom and creating expectations with your needs? Are you canceling all the right reasons and activating all the wrong reasons?

A Relationship Is a Mirror of Your Self

First, a relationship is a mirror for your Self. Secondly, it helps you to grow, because in a relationship you are to make decisions, you are to experience, you are to say "yes," and you are to say "no." How many of you do not dare to say "no" in your relationship? And how can you say "yes" if you do not know how to say "no"? The "yes" and "no" are to be balanced.

I have noticed that as soon as you move into a relationship, you think of the *timing* of the relationship, of the long-term. You want to hold on to your relationship, to make it long-term. What is this? What is the fear behind this? If you are in a relationship freely, then you will receive a great deal. When you give, for example, without even knowing that you are giving, the relationship is fulfilling. When you are in a relationship and do not expect the other person to change, then you are growing.

Remember that in a true relationship there is no "must," "should," or obligation. Commit yourself to your Higher Self in your relationship without expecting the other person to commit himself or herself to you. A relationship is an opportunity—it takes you into "relation," to relate, to the Creation itself. Your soul has taken you there.

And you have attracted this mirror. This person that you attract to you is your own mirror, so if someday you feel hate, disgust, or jealousy, and say to yourself, "I wish I had never been in this relationship," you are facing *yourself*. If you choose, however, to move into a relationship where it's only glory, only victory, only Oneness, only Unity, and Divinity, then the sharing will be so magnificent and so powerful that the breath that you both breathe will merge with the whole universe. I am convinced of this. Experience it joyously.

When in this relationship, take time to know if you are loving *you* in the relationship or if you are forgetting you. Forgetting yourself is quite a big mistake. Love *you* in the relationship, and you won't constantly go outside of *yourself* and love only the other. When you forget your Self, how do you think the relationship is going to enrich itself?

And there is the *image* of yourself that you are bringing forth in this relationship, the part of *yourself* that you are bringing forth. This is a very important point—examining your self-image.

It is also important to question your purpose in life, whether you are growing, and whether you are aware. You may find you are loving, but ask yourself if you are loving the Higher Self in the other person or loving the body. Ask yourself if you are *in fact* loving, if you are inviting. Or are you confusing the body and the Self? Where there is confusion, reflect on what kind of confusion this relationship is activating in you.

Still, understand that you are to be in a relationship with your Higher Self first, taking care of the Divinity in *you* in this relationship. Be aware of what you are practicing and see if you are using your relationship to glorify inner Love with the Self, with Self knowledge. Ask yourself if you are praising you, glorifying you, *you* as the Higher Self.

Consider whether or not you are choosing this opportunity to be humble and if you are choosing this opportunity to better know *who you are* through the relationship. For example, question whether you are choosing this opportunity to allow your fears to come up and if you are facing those fears, if you are choosing your relationship to experience yourself naked. What are you choosing?

And in this relationship, ask yourself if you are demonstrating your Higher Self. When you are sincere, when you are true with your Self, whatever you are practicing in your relationship (meaning you *and* your partner) will become only Oneness. You and your partner will then be one.

Again, when you long for a relationship, it is because you have forgotten yourself. You have forgotten your Higher Self. You have lost yourself, and you're looking for you *through somebody else*. I suggest that you who are choosing to move into a relationship ask yourself what this partner is going to *fill* inside you. I use that word on purpose, because many of you feel there is something missing inside you, and you wish to *fill* in that missing piece.

So the questions arising are, "Whom do I truly love? Do I know what Love is?" It is important to know if there is truth in your heart in this relationship and, if there is, *where* is the truth of it? Ask yourself if you are falling into a pit, falling in love, in passion, and if this is a positive experience. The words that I am using, whether right or wrong, positive or negative, are just to give you an idea of the teaching, for you to understand. Know that there is no right, no wrong.

Most of you are longing for a Love that you have wanted from your mother or father and have not yet experienced, although your first relationship is to be with *yourself*—the first one. If you have not moved into this chapter of your life yet, I invite you to do so. Then when you choose to move into a relationship with yourself, question whether or not you are the body, the mind, or the experience. It is important to know if you are evolving in this relationship.

Of course, you are to see your relationship as sacred. This relationship is a huge opportunity for you to magnify your Love for yourself. Do you know how selfish a relationship is? It is so selfish when you don't love the other. It's very selfish unless there is an exceptionally high frequency of Love and vibration in your relationship.

Also, consider the role of the Supreme Self in your relationship.[1] Question the role of Divinity in it, whether or not you are conscious, and if it is possible to receive from another person the Love you are longing for.

Be aware that if you do not love yourself, it is impossible for you to love your partner; and if you live in fear, you cannot experience the Love of your partner. If, when you meet a being, you say, "We are in this relationship. Promise me that it is forever, that we will live together and you will look only at me and that you will not love anybody else," know that this is not Love. Most of you do not see your value. Most of you are reproaching yourselves. So, if you travel with this baggage, how can you experience the relationship? No, it is not possible.

As soon as you feel jealousy, for example, know that in your relationship you have a fear of losing your partner. Ask yourself why you have this fear. It is because you know that you are not giving yourself one-hundred percent to your partner, so now your partner can receive—meaning your partner can receive from someone else—what you are not giving.

Now let's say that you and your partner are living together and you share everything. This is your ideal: The charming prince or princess comes to you, and life is so perfect. It's not true; you are just not experiencing truth, but let's say it is like this. You are living together and you tell your partner everyday that you love him or her. Then your partner does something that you don't like. How do you feel? By doing that "something" that you do not like—maybe it's going to the theater, to a spiritual conference, or spending five days with a guru—you feel abandoned the moment your partner makes this decision. You feel that he or she is rejecting you, is not seeing your value, and does not respect you.

And let's also say that your partner has just met someone and is deeply in love. He or she *thinks* they are deeply in love, that they are *falling* in love. That is their illusion. And then your partner decides to tell you of meeting this someone and of wanting a relationship with this new person. What would you feel? Well, you would cry and you would probably hate your partner for a few minutes or months or maybe years. You wouldn't want to see him or her.

This is all about manipulation. In a relationship, most of you are trying to *get* something. And when your partner is not ready to give it to you, you are not happy. And that's what you want—whatever the person *doesn't* want to give you is exactly what you want. So stop this behavior. This is not a true relationship; this is commerce, like when you give money and receive something in return. You must not be like this with your partner.

Honor Your True Feelings of Love

Be true to yourself. Look at your behavior. Look at your patterns and you will know one thing: No matter how much you tell your partner you love him or her, your partner will not trust you one-hundred percent because your partner has not experienced his or her own Love for himself or herself. That's the way it is. As soon as you tell your partner you love him or her, in your partner's mind it will be, "Oh, my God, does he, does she really love me?"

When your partner doesn't believe in your love, you will be asked to prove your love. And in that moment, you will start changing your attitude, the way you function, your behavior; you will start to do what your partner is asking of you. And at the same time, your partner will also change his or her natural way of functioning, of being, and all of this will begin changing both of you.

Behind all of this there is fear. Will he or she still love me if I do this, if I speak like this? And this is where you start losing the relationship, in all these little details of everyday life, because this is where you are losing your Self. You are no longer honoring your Higher Self, and there is less attraction to the Love. You are not expansive anymore, not open or blossoming anymore, because there is fear behind everything.

On the other hand, suppose you finally accept that this being loves you that much. Then you will say, "Oh, my God, I wonder if it will last. This is so beautiful. It can't be true. You know, Sai Maa, it will not last. I can feel it will not last because it's so beautiful." This is your behavior; this is your pattern. The moment you're in love, the moment you realize this being loves you, you experience fear, the fear of losing. And this is where you separate yourself from your partner.

Is it clear that, when you love him or her so much that you forget yourself, you also forget to honor your Higher Self? Ask yourself, is it possible for a relationship to blossom, to unfold, when you're not honoring yourself? How is that possible? Then the relationship is moving only in one direction. So I ask you to ponder, to contemplate, what a relationship is for, why you create a relationship—if not *to blossom*.

My Precious Ones, it is very, very easy to know when you are in the truth: The relationship will uplift you, and the feelings will uplift you. Feelings that are from the truth will uplift you, expand you, and shift you into a state of inner joy, a certain delight that is real, that is from *within*. It's not coming from your partner—it's coming from your own experience. This is where a relationship is meant to take each individual.

Sai Maa with Ms. Dana Blank, superintendent of the Indiana Women's Prison.

5

Forgiveness Brings Freedom

Forgiveness is a doorway to freedom,

and this freedom serves to move you

into higher consciousness.

Forgiveness Brings Freedom

When the Mind Forgives, the Heart Forgives

Forgiveness is of great importance in sadhana. As you probably know, joy is a key, but forgiveness is also a key. Forgiveness is a doorway to freedom, and this freedom serves to move you into higher consciousness. So many times I think of what Jesus went through, how he was treated and how he forgave. Such freedom, such release of judgment! Forgiveness is to be at the center of your sadhana, the center of your life. Tremendous power is in the act of forgiveness.

The moment the mind chooses to forgive, in that place where resentment is felt, the heart forgives. Then more Love penetrates the heart chakra and more Light penetrates the heart chakra. The Higher Self is always ready to pour more Grace into your life and free the personality, because life is to be a life of mercy, compassion, naturalness, and forgiveness. Thus, whenever you cannot forgive, you are to question yourself.

It is important to choose in which state you wish to live. For example, if you say, "I wish peace on the planet," then how can you live without forgiving? To move into that state of the peaceful mind, your ego is to be transformed into

Love and Light. Resentment is connected to dense forces that will influence the subtle bodies, particularly the emotional body and the mental body. These are the main bodies to be purified to carry more Light, to carry more peace on this plane, and to move into higher frequencies. Of course, your ego is connected to these two bodies and also to the physical, gross body.

For such a long time, your ego has been fed by lower emotions. Then suddenly, because you are on the moksha (liberation) path and moving toward enlightenment,[1] you are saying to the Higher Self, "Please take over so the outer personality and the ego don't keep directing everything." The ego doesn't like this because in this situation the ego sees its end. So the ego moves into a revolution, the state of mind where it usually takes on all of the lower emotions and denser frequencies of pain, resentment, anger, frustration, envy, and jealousy.

So it is your duty to activate the attributes of God, purity, and obedience, so that the Higher Self can come forth. At the beginning of the process, this is a fight and you may even have doubts. Naturally doubt will arise, as the ego wishes to win, but you must be strong and persevere so that the power of Light that you carry, this great divine power, will be realized.

Love is power. Do not doubt this. Even if doubt comes, accept it, but know as a master you are not to doubt the higher powers. The angels and devas are always ready to assist. Remember, because of free will, ascended masters, gurus, and angels will not touch your energy, will not interfere unless you ask for their help.

It is time for you to take command of your life and be responsible for your own actions. Do not allow the ego to manipulate you any longer. Because you have been weak for such a very long time, the samskaras (past experiences stored in the mind) will tend to remain in lower frequencies, but be courageous.[2] Courage is necessary, so do not give up. Do *not* give up.

If you wish to be free from pain, use discernment. Again, move to your heart. Do not give power to your ego anymore. Allow the Self, the Higher Self, to express itself, to be of service to you. All this old karma was planted long ago, and now the trees and the fruits of that karma are appearing. Start now to sow different seeds, and you will no longer feel guilt or shame. Thus, anger will not have the power to continue to grow.

Of course, forgiving *yourself* is a must, and asking for forgiveness brings humility. Start to control, to master, your emotions and your lower feelings. Be aware. Observe yourself and start diving into the path. Observe your thought patterns. Change. Shift. You have the capacity, and by choosing righteousness, you will naturally move into higher frequencies. These higher feelings will bring much more joy to your life.

Keep forgiving. Train your mind to shift. Know that your mind is a very powerful tool and it's also an "empty space," so whatever you put in it *will be powerful*, because it is a powerful space. The mind doesn't know if what is put into it is negative or positive, because there is no discernment in the mind—it's like an empty space and it's very powerful. So whatever you put there will grow, and grow very strongly; therefore, being positive is very important.

And the more you are positive, the more you will *be* positive, because the same energy you put in your mind will go through your whole body via the blood. In this way you can say the mind is all over the body, just as your mental body is all around you. This means that if you choose now to plant a seed of positivity, it will begin to grow, and when your Higher Self sees what you are doing, it will support you.

When the ascended masters see what you are doing, they will support you as you put more Light into your subtle bodies.[3] This is when you are enlightening yourself. If you are truly dedicated to the Light, motivated, disciplined, and pure, then the law of attraction will come to you. It does not take long to be enlightened. Pour Light into your whole being constantly. A great deal of separation will drop and the state of ananda (bliss) will begin to be realized.

Again, remember about choice. Choose whether you serve the highest or the ego. Activate the law of forgiveness as much as you wish. Enlightenment is in your hands. You cannot complain that you do not have Grace for enlightenment. I realize that many of you say you *want* enlightenment, *but* you do not *choose* enlightenment. So again, what is your choice? If you say, I want this, and you choose something else, don't blame anyone. Open your heart, forgive, choose, and transformation will take place.

You will love and you will feel loved as well. Every day you will feel more joy, and you will open gateways to your Higher Self. When your Self comes closer, there is naturally more joy. In contrast, the ego closes those gateways. So are you inviting your Godhead to come closer into your personal life, into your personality?

With Love, you can raise your vibration easily. Many inner tools are available. The breath, the angels, the ascended masters—these are what will take you into the *"one-moment,"* into the *"now."* If you wish to fully experience yourself, to experience your own potential, you have only one choice: Merge with your Higher Self. Only Love will attract your Higher Self. There is not one technique on the planet besides Love that will attract your I AM Presence to you, to your personality. When you are free, you will love easily.

Remember, it is easy to move into old patterns, so be aware. Be willing to live in the Light. Your ego will give you feelings and emotions to make you think it's right. Most of the time the ego likes to justify, coming in different ways to make you feel that it's exactly what you need. Your ego intends to keep you in a lower vibration, in lower frequencies, always manipulating your senses.

Be aware. It is your duty to master yourself. It is your duty to *choose*. Rise above these emotions, for only then will glory be experienced. Master your senses and consciousness will shift. Then you will no longer be feeding lower vibrations. Patterns will drop. Then you are choosing freedom, and forgiveness becomes an easy process.

Feeding emotions with your mind is weakness and it weakens your senses. When you forgive, you can easily live with no conditions and love with no conditions. You can live more fully in the present, in the "now." The ego will then see that it is not being fed anymore. Still, self-inquiry is important. Do not hesitate to check your feelings to see if they are coming from fear or from Love. Shift gears whenever it is needed. Choice. Awareness and choice.

Often when you forgive, you think you are right with the Self. Well, you do not have to win or lose—no right, no wrong. Just be completely transparent and forgive for the sake of forgiveness. Love for the sake of Love.

Sai Maa in the Grand Tetons, Wyoming, where she traveled to work with the Ascended Master energies that reside in this mountain range.

6

The Nature of the Mind

The mind is able to think because

of the Self, because the

Light of the Self is shining through.

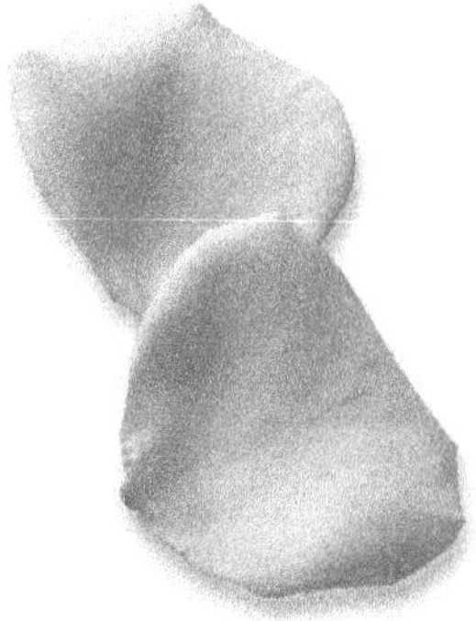

The Nature of the Mind

Train the Mind to Go Within

If you truly choose to deal with the mind, you *must* turn within and allow the Shakti to awaken your own inner power. Only then are you mastering your mind. Your mind has its own Grace, but when your thoughts become your only world, you get caught in that falsehood. This mind is your best friend and your worst enemy, so this mind can be a huge obstacle that can prevent you from knowing your Self. Your mind can hide your Higher Self from you, can veil the Self—such is the power of the mind.

If you were to free your mind, its Grace would reveal itself, but your mind makes you feel you are unworthy, that you have to worry, and that you are far from God. It gives you this sense of separateness, *but* know that this same mind when well fed will serve to unite you with the Higher Self. This mind is the cause of bondage as well as the cause of liberation, duality as well as freedom, bad as well as good, wrong as well as right, and sadness as well as joy.

At a certain point, it is very, very important to study and know the mind. When you ask yourself who is making the mind function, is it not the Self? So the Self is shining through the mind, but that does not mean that the mind knows the Self. No! The mind always goes to external affairs, always; the *external* is the concern of the mind. The mind has forgotten how to go inward, how to merge with the Self and radiate its Light and Love. This is the reason why you are to meditate—to master the mind and to train your mind to go within. Only in that quietness will the senses disappear, will the Self shine forth. Then you are tapping into your Divinity, into the "now," into the present, the Presence.[1]

The value of the mind is unspeakable, infinite. I'm sure you know that if the mind is gone, everything is gone. This is the value, the power of the mind. The Grace of the mind is necessary, so ask your guru or teacher and you'll receive this Grace. When your mind is strong and quiet, no worldly thing can touch your being. The value of a good, healthy mind is beyond words. The purer your mind, the better you'll feel. You will experience the greatest joy the moment your mind is still, then no more agitation, no more restlessness. Know that a turbulent mind is a weak mind, but when your mind is still, you live with great power. No other situation will give you this joy. The joy of the still mind is the Self.

Now, do *not* go after the mind to control it—it will get worse. It will control *you* and then you are lost. Understand it, feed it, nourish it, know it, and then only stillness will be experienced. The mind is but a vibration, a contracted form of pure consciousness, of the Self, of the same Self that has created the universe. It's the pure energy of Creation.

As a contracted part of consciousness, this mind creates infinite thoughts, just as consciousness creates universes. Consciousness takes the form of mind and thoughts, and then you create your own world. It is your world that you have in your mind, and this world is unreal and untrue. *And* most of the time you are afraid of the power of your mind. Your world is then a mind-made world: temporary, personal, memories all enclosed within the mind and hanging by a thread.

When a mind is not steady, then nothing in it is steady. The mind's nature is to roam about, but you are the master who is to shift your focus and go to the space *beyond* the mind, to pure consciousness. I invite you to refuse all thoughts which do not fit you. In this manner, stay only with the I AM Presence. Anything else, drop it. Of course, the mind will rebel in the beginning, but keep your focus, persevere, be patient, do not give up, witness, and be one with the real Self. Your real Self is not restless, but is peace, Love, and Light. It's only the Self's reflection in the mind that *appears* restless because the mind is restless.

Identify Your Fears

The time has come to move your being to greater clarity, greater Love. To do so, you must face, resolve, and transmute what stands in the way—fear. Remember, my role is to lead you to face whatever is in your way, so that you can see these obstacles in a different light. See the *illusion* of fear, the *immaturity* of meanings you place on emotional reactions, and the *smallness* of these perceived obstacles.

If, however, you keep choosing the same old thought forms and behavior patterns, I can do nothing except love you. Yes, the ego-you has the exceptional ability to refine the same old thing as if it were new. I tell you, it's often the same old thing with a new face. Be wary. This "newness" you consider growth is mostly a trick or manipulation of the ego-mind, an ego-survival mechanism.

If you are sincere, I have a request: Put your fears front and center. Spend time identifying as precisely as possible what your fears, concerns, and obstacles are. Move them out of your body and through your mind. Once they are clear to you, it would even be good to speak them (the fears, concerns, and obstacles) out loud to the universe. Be sure to identify the one that looms largest. Again, be as precise as possible. Your clarity has a direct bearing on what will be accomplished.

The Mind Has Its Own Grace

Yes, the mind has its own Grace. The mind is a contracted aspect of consciousness, and consciousness is Grace. All in the universe is created out of Grace. The difference between the Self and the mind is that the Self shines by its own Light, whereas the mind and the ego are separate, yet sparkles of Light, of consciousness, also illuminate them.

The mind is able to *think* because of the Self, because the Light of the Self is shining through. Read about the Self and you will know who you are. With the Grace of the Self, the mind can "think"—ask for this Grace of the Self. The Self is the knower, the Witness.

Thoughts are like clouds in the sky; they come and they go. The sky is not affected. Just as with your mirror: Some days you offer a nice smiling, joyful face to the mirror, and some days you offer a depressed face to the mirror. Is the mirror affected? *No.* In the same way, the vastness, the consciousness, the Self, or the Absolute, in you is "all ways" present and never affected by any of this. Then it becomes simple. Do not pay attention to the thoughts. Focus on the Absolute and the mind will calm down by itself, because you will not pay attention to it any more. Then the Higher Self will reveal itself to you. It's natural for the Self to reveal itself to you.

If you are using a mantra such as *I AM Light, So Ham* (I AM), or *Om Namah Shivaya* (I honor the Divine within me), use it in your inhale and your exhale and listen to your breath. I promise that in a short period of time you'll get the juice of your meditation. The mantra takes you to your inner world.[2] Your mind will still itself if you keep your body and senses still, so keep the body still. Also keep your spine straight—this is very important—to steady the mind.

Silence the Mind

God is right in front of you. Look and see God. Yes, meditate. Be serene, be joyous, allowing this joy to transform what is to be transformed. The reason for meditation is to experience the truth within, to discover the Eternal within, and to receive darshan (a blessing) of the Divine within. Then in living your life, attach yourself to this Divinity, totally.

Beloveds, you do not meditate to be realized. You are already realized. It is to calm your mind, this mind that binds you. The mind is so strong that it gets in the way, with a new thought every fraction of a second. When you agree with the thoughts you are happy, and when you doubt the thoughts, you feel miserable. Again you are trapped.

Be joyous. This is the key!

One day a being called to say, "Sai Maa, I am so happy. I am going to live with so-and-so." "Oh," I replied. "Do you know him?" "Yes, Sai Maa, he is so nice." "Do you know yourself?" I asked. Silence. Only her breathing could be heard. You see how fragile and weak we are. It is only the mind.

Recently, I spent one hour at the ocean looking at the waves, waves rolling like thoughts falling in the mind. The mind leads our lives, always wanting, always doing.

Yes, Beloveds, the worst as well as the best is in the mind; it is a matter of choice. Do you choose the best or the worst? What do you choose to achieve? Your mind will try to keep you away from the Divine. So master your mind, silence your mind, because you cannot trust the mind. Allow the Grace of the Divine to remove the tendencies of the mind so you will experience your inner freedom.

7

The Transformative Power of Meditation

Feed the mind on higher truth,

taste divine Presence,

and be in Love with God.

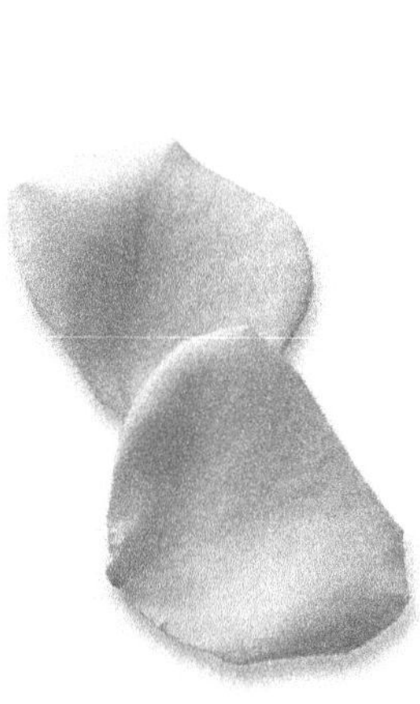

The Transformative Power of Meditation

All Limitations Vanish

Meditation is a natural state, a real experience that allows you to discover your inner being. When you sit for meditation, do not do anything. The feeling of joy comes naturally. Always start your meditation with an absolute feeling of conviction to cherish your own divine Light. It's a moment when you enter your own being, your own inner heart.

Meditation is grand. Through meditation you realize who you are. Meditate with Love. Through meditation your consciousness shifts. It can be very subtle, but you can notice the shift in your everyday activities. It's only during meditation that you see your own inner Light shine brighter and brighter. Through meditation all limitations vanish. The body-mind shifts, and then your virtues are experienced. The mind also experiences a life shift.

Not a single moment of meditation is the same. You may even think nothing is happening. Dear Ones, know that something *is* happening. As soon as you start to meditate, your inner being starts to unfold. You cannot stop that process. When you meditate, the inner spiritual power starts to uplift you.

This power transforms you on many different levels, and through this spiritual knowledge your enlightenment begins.

Meditation has its own power, its own Grace. You may invoke the power, the Grace, after sitting silently. As soon as you become aware, there is a glow, a flow, and a liberation—then your energy is different.

The Purpose of Meditation

The purpose of meditation is to experience inner joy, inner peace, and inner contentment. All our senses are quiet—only their bliss, Sat-Chit-Ananda (existence-consciousness-bliss), is experienced.

Instead of thinking negative thoughts, breathe the awareness "I AM loved, I AM pure, I AM bliss, I AM That!" Cultivation of dharma within and without is the root of all joy.

Dive Deep Within

Once true joy, peace, Love, and contentment are unveiled in your world, then the world will be seen through different glasses. You may even pretend to be angry, and yet inside, serene joy and Love will be bubbling up.

For Love and joy, remember only one thing: Dive deep within. These are your own inner treasures, and no one—absolutely no one—can take them away from you. These attributes are the power of the Higher Self, and they will naturally filter into your everyday life. Then you will know only of giving. Your heart will soak in that divine abundance that is powerfully streaming into the universe. Then you will be in bliss and you will become intoxicated, because this state is the very state of the nature of God or Source. This bliss is embedded in every single atom. Open your vision to experience supreme, abundant, divine, graceful consciousness and you'll receive everything.

To experience Divinity, you *have* to avoid distractions because you can't have both. It's one or the other. Afterwards you will receive all without asking for it. You are to transcend this world while still engaging in ordinary worldly activities and responsibilities. Focus on the Self. Be centered *"all ways."* By the Grace of the Self, this world can be glorified; for that, you are to choose nonattachment.

Sometimes I watch several of you. You wish to rise to the nobility of your Higher Self, but you spend your time with low-minded people who control you, who manipulate you, and who are obsessed with their artificial values. Move fearlessly in your sadhana and be strong. This is a path that requires constant vigilance, constant awareness to discern which choices are appropriate, which radical changes are for the best.

Go deep within. After work when you are at home, be in silence. Do not overdo it. There are treasures inside. Feed the mind on higher truth, taste divine Presence, and be in Love with God. If you love your guru, see your guru as your most Beloved. The illusion of mind must burn in the fire of your practice.

Mantra, the Vibration of God

What is a mantra? A mantra is a set of sacred syllables evoking a divine being or it is the name of God. Mantras are unique and very powerful. They are words that are infused with power, divine power. Mantras have such impact that they heal and mostly calm the mind. The more you focus on the mantra, the more you receive from it. A mantra is God as word, as sound, and as vibration. And because God is your essence, using a mantra consciously helps you to move toward God. A mantra repeated in total faith takes you *to* God, and you can experience God realization.

It is important to surrender to the mantra, to love the mantra, and to love the deity with total faith, without doubt. Repeat the name of God with full concentration so you can realize your soul. When the mantra is given by a guru, they add their Shakti and activate the mantra. Seize this opportunity, as the Love of this being is precious, and receiving such a mantra is rare. The power of the Shakti will definitely serve you.

Ask yourself the question, "What am I ready to give to the mantra?" Are you committed to the mantra? Remember, a mantra is the vibration, the formless form, of God. The mantra will bring your mind to focus on the Light. Sometimes mantras are given with specific directions, so please respect them. Practice these directions, be sincere, be willing to change, and be willing to allow the mind to be enlightened by the Light of the mantra.

The bhakti (the devotion of the seeker) is of great importance in the repetition of the mantra.[1] You may say the mantra aloud, but know also that some mantras are to be repeated silently. Be fully aware. Be in the "now" when it's said. The more you repeat the mantra, the more the mantra becomes a part of you, and you move closer and closer to it. Say your mantra as much as possible, the name of God always on the tongue, so that you think only divine thoughts and speak only divine words.

Finally it becomes natural, and you include the mantra in all activities. The mantra brings a lot of Love, joy, peace, and strength as you experience the peak of your sadhana. With the mantra you'll go deeper and deeper. Enjoy the cosmic ecstasy of God as you.

The Power of the Mantra

The mantra is one of the most important factors of sadhana, the basis of your practice—I will even say the root of everything you do or see on this plane as well as in the universe. The mantra is a divine sound, the sound of and from Mother-Father Creator. Sound . . . sound . . . it may be music, chants, wind, birds, human sounds, water, drumming, toning, or your *breath.*

Mantras are made of divine letters as well as divine sound. Your *inhale* is "So," your *exhale* is "Ham," such beauty, such abundance, such divine sound, the power of your inner sound, the power of So Ham, the power of sound to create the universe, manifesting universes by sound. Have you ever thought of the use of sound and letters on this plane?[2] A mantra is the whole being of the Supreme, of the Self, of God.

You cannot miss the boat that takes you to liberation if you say your mantra *consciously, in total devotion.* This is the quickest way to merge with God, the quickest and easiest when japa is practiced. Then you can only practice good actions and thoughts can only be divine, because in your life your focus is "all ways" *the name* and *the word.*

A mantra carries its power, its full potential, in the whole universe. The point is this: How do you repeat these powerful mantras? Are you absorbed in them, or is japa a habit while your mind practices something else? Ask yourself if you truly understand the real meaning, the real understanding, of mantras. Are you *aware*? Are you conscious?

Now ask yourself if you, in fact, identify with the mantra. Do you truly activate the mantra and breathe the mantra? The power of mantras can transform a being if the right *understanding* is practiced. Mantras can only take you in one clear direction; they assist you to transcend and to be one with the Transcendent.

Using a mantra consciously is a great, a divine, and a powerful detergent for *your whole being,* for the physical blood as well as your subtle bodies. Depression can easily disappear with japa practice, and blood can be washed clean with japa. Know that the power of God is in the mantra. Now if there is a lack of faith, the mantra will do nothing. But no language can express the power of words transmitted by masters, by gurus, *to a real, true seeker!*

When a mantra is divinizing your mind—such Shakti is in the mantra—how can your consciousness stay the same? And how many samskaras can be dissolved just by japa? The mantra is alive and has the ability, the capacity, and the responsibility to transform your mind, your coarse qualities, and your negative thought forms into a totally divinized being.

Do not tell me you've been repeating your mantra for a long time but with no results. Is it an inert or a living mantra? Some of you come to me and say, "I've changed my guru, Sai Maa. What mantra *should I use now?*" Dear Ones, mantras are *not* like clothes. You do *not* change your mantra every day or whenever the personality *wants* to change. The name of God is the name of God!

Very often after receiving a mantra you feel it's a new beginning. Strength, power, beauty, security, bliss, Grace, and more occur actively in your inner consciousness. The Shakti that was waiting is now active in you; the movement, the Permanent, the Self, and the Godhead all start to be active. You are *born.*

I invite you to be consciously addicted to the mantra. Begin like this: Eat it, drink it, play with it, think of it, and love it. In everything there is the mantra, everywhere the mantra. Whatever you see is the mantra; whatever you hear or say is the mantra. Imagine you are going up on the roof, choosing to go higher. You are on the ground, so you need a ladder in your spiritual practice. What is your ladder? The mantra.

Use your mantra to live in higher consciousness, to be closer to the Self. See no difference between the mantra and your Higher Self. The mantra has the power fully to divinize the organs, the glands, the subtle bodies, the speech, and the whole being, until you rest in pure consciousness again. In the meantime, you may hear this mantra being repeated by *itself* inside you.

Often you ask how to do japa, how to repeat your mantra. Bring your mind consciousness to the tip of your tongue—this is a high-frequency vibration. From the tongue the vibrations move into the throat chakra, to the heart chakra, and then continue to other chakras. There is a point where the mantra permeates your whole being, and then every word you pronounce at that instant is *a mantra!* Even if you scold someone, it's a mantra. When a human uses her or his own Shakti and that Shakti transmits, penetrates, and enters the seeker or disciple, his or her existence will never, ever be the same. It's *a new world!*

There is "before the mantra" and "after the mantra." After using the mantra your inner consciousness will be active instead of dormant. To truly enjoy your sadhana, the mind and body are to be pure; only then are you living in ananda. Mantras purify the mind and body. We often work with *Om Namah Shivaya.* This mantra will purify in no time—results are quick.

Allow your mantra, the power of your mantra, to expand its power in each cell of your body. Allow your mantra to saturate your mind and heart. The mantra is a living power, prana, and life force. Your mantra is the Self, and it will definitely transcend the individual consciousness to Self consciousness, to truth. This is the role of the mantra.

Repeat your mantra with Love and the fruits are pure delight, pure bliss. You can pass through this worldly existence with great ease, with total faith and Love.

With Courage, Step into the Unknown

Meditate. Be silent. Keep the mantra *So Ham* on the breath until you are lost. The mantra will take you to that place from which it comes, the Supreme within.

In this victory of Love, our Oneness will be remembered. The greatness of "remembrance" comes from the depth of your heart.

With courage step into the unknown, that place where you have no reference. The All That Is, is in that space—the Oneness, Unity, freedom, bliss, Love, Light, and *real life.* Many experiences will come. Do not be attached to any of them. Keep meditating. Many colors of light will come—go beyond them all. Go to that place where there is "no thing," nothing. This is the place.

Meditate on the Divine

Beloved Souls,

> Pure Love is Divine Love,
> It's God's Love.
> God's Love is Grace,
> God's Love is Power,
> God's nature is Love,
> God's Love is compassion.
> God "all ways" looks at you
> With eyes of Love.
> Be God.
> Look at others and
> Yourself with eyes of Love.
> God is Pure.
> Self is Pure.

This purity is inside each of you, no matter who you are: ignorant beggar, professor, maid. Meditate on that purity, on that Divinity. You will be permeated by that which you meditate on with Love.

Seek, make an effort. You'll find the treasure. You carry your Higher Self wherever you go, so it's very easy to meditate on That. Wherever you are, meditate. It does not matter who you are or what you've done. Meditate on your Self. Freedom and liberation lie in meditation, in the only place where you master the mind and actually meet yourself.

You are going everywhere to find peace. You go here and there because you do not know your true value, your own perfection. Always remember the Lord. You'll receive everything from the Self; you'll receive the experience of knowledge. From meditation on your Self, you will become a lover of God. Meditate with a deep feeling of Love, of purity, and of surrender. This is Grace.

So many times you tell me you are very happy because you are in love with X or Y, and it lasts a few days, weeks, or months. Then you are sad. I suggest that you be in Love with life in its fullness. Be in Love with life and you will *never* be sad. Trust me; meditate. Within each of you lies a tremendous power of Love and joy and an ocean of bliss. To experience that state in its fullness, you are to be still in body and mind; you are to meditate. Do nothing so that this state, this consciousness, reveals itself to you.

Be Aware of This Presence

It is fine to have visions, *but* it is not necessary, *not at all.* You do not meditate for a vision; you meditate for peace. Most important is the innate tranquility, the inner joy. Everything is so quiet and bliss arises by itself. The only awareness is to be in "the moment," in the precious "now."

In that consciousness described, you experience bliss for no outside reason. It's coming from your own Self, your own Divinity, your own Presence, from your inner you. Keep honoring your Self, and be aware of this Presence. This is God.

Dr. Pankaj Naram and Sai Maa being playful with His Holiness the Dalai Lama.

8

Awaken to the Truth of Your Being

See yourself as the Christ Light,
as the Light of Buddha, Moses, Mohammed, and
all the great ones. This is the truth. Own it.

Awaken to the Truth of Your Being

Know You Are the Embodiment of God

Human beings spend their time looking outwards. They forget the temple of God inside the heart. Now is the time to go within, to connect within, and to explore. Now is the time to step into mastery. Now is the time to be pure radiance, to radiate your Love, to radiate your truth.

It is time to consciously anchor the divine qualities that are within you. Consciously call forth all you have ever hoped to be. Call that forth from within yourself and anchor it as reality. Everything is within you: abundance, wisdom, truth, Light, and healing energy for yourself and others. It is all within you.

So know that everything you see in me is possible for you; it is yours to be, but you must *claim* it. It is yours to share, but you must *radiate* it. It is all about consciousness and awareness; it is all about opening, receiving, activating, anchoring, and owning. This life is all about *you*. It is not about others. It is not about so many of the things that you are attached to. It is about you finding who you are, expressing who you are, and owning who you are. Nothing in your mind will help you to understand the reality and truth of your being. It is mighty. It is huge.

Say to yourself,

I AM the Embodiment of God.
I AM the Embodiment of God.
I AM the Embodiment of God.

I AM the Resurrection and the Life.
I AM the Resurrection and the Life.
I AM the Resurrection and the Life.

I AM Truth.
I AM Love.
I AM Abundance.
I AM All that there is.

Let divine joy fill you. Let divine Love fill you. Let divine peace be your reality.

Know that there is no separation. It is your choice that creates separation. It is not reality. Visualize yourself as the sacred fire. See yourself as the flames of the sacred fire. Go inside your heart to the "permanent atom," find the "blue flame" in your heart, and spread that through your entire body. Bring it into your organs, glands, and chakras, and feel it burn in your brain. Extend it out through all your subtle bodies and into your aura.

See yourself as the sacred fire and know this is the truth. See yourself as the Christ Light, as the Light of Buddha, Moses, Mohammed, and all the great ones. This is the truth. Own it.

Now, consciously *identify with* the reality you choose to embody in this lifetime. Consciously *call forth* the truth you choose to embody in this lifetime.

Consciously *anchor* the reality you choose to call forth in this lifetime. I AM That I AM.[1] I AM the Embodiment of God. I AM the sacred fire of Christ's Love. I AM the universe. Use this teaching: I AM That, Thou Art That, All this is nothing but That.

Discipline is a doorway to this mastery. Awareness is a doorway to mastery. Devotion is also a doorway to mastery. Ask and the door shall be opened. Your spiritual guides can bring you almost all the way, but you must choose to walk through the door. Awareness. Choice. Be *in* the world, but not *of* this world. Be a being of Light, but do not be bound by this reality, this third-dimensional reality. Be a multidimensional being. And don't try to fill the void from an unhappy childhood. Don't try to find what you did not receive in childhood, as if you lack something. It is all within you. The Love you are looking for is yours to give *yourself.*

You do not need anyone to love you. You are Love at your essence. Love is all you are. You are swimming in an ocean of Love, and you are shot full of Love. You are swimming in an ocean of Light, shot full of Light. You are swimming in an ocean of abundance, shot full with abundance. You are swimming in an ocean of pure Shakti, pure energy, shot full of energy, full of Shakti. You are consciousness in an ocean of consciousness.

You are the embodiment of God, remembering. Questions can be very helpful at this time. Ask yourself, "What is real? What is true?" Do not get caught in habits. Do not get caught in belief systems. Do not limit the truth of who you are. Do not limit yourself to *your body or your senses.* That is all third-dimensional reality. Pierce the veils of ignorance, and be aware of the sacred fire, of Mother Kundalini Shakti.[2] Bring this Shakti up from the base chakra through all your chakras to the crown chakra. Bring the Shakti up above the head, all the way up to your I AM Presence. You are to open to That, to express That.

This is awareness and choice. Awareness and choice.

Sai Maa at Lake Titicaca in Peru, during a trip to South America where she travelled to perform planetary healing work.

9

Sadhana, the Path to Grace

The more you live in the vibration of God,

the more divine vibrations will

emanate from your being.

Sadhana, the Path to Grace

Moving Into Purity

Sadhana is a practice, a practice of inner world and outer world, a practice of moving from one world to another. It's a moment-to-moment attitude, a practice of disciplining yourself physically and mentally. By your sadhana, your practice, you will realize you are *in* this world but not *of* this world. You can live better *in* this world. You can improve your way of living, a refined quality, by seeing from within. It's also awareness.

In your sadhana you can include contemplation, concentration, meditation, chanting, silence, and exercise such as yoga. Sadhana makes you strong, purifies your being, your whole being—you move from the gross to the subtle. It's a spiritual way of living, and you become aware of your goal or mission in life during sadhana.

A lot of contentment is also experienced during sadhana, contentment which is coming from deep within, from the God within, the God that is you. This contentment is amrit. It rejuvenates you, reenergizes you, reenergizes your whole body, and intensifies your Love, your Love for the Divine. This contentment creates the state or feeling of being a devotee, then later a disciple, of spirit. Faith increases and your whole being—subtle, mental, and physical bodies—gets stronger.

The Supreme Being Within

Develop faith in your sadhana. Through sadhana you easily experience the master you are, because with these disciplines you master your senses. You become a witness to the maya and the drama of this worldly existence. There is such power in that contentment that it then starts infusing your every action and thought. Your experience of life is then transformed.

There is also abundance in sadhana. It's a gateway to Grace, a gateway that can be opened. The more joy you allow yourself to be in, the more the gateway opens itself. This is the tremendous power of Grace. Grace bestows a sublime state of joy that takes you to the Transcendent. The Transcendent grants you the Shakti to transcend worldly attachments, which you engage out of ignorance, not discerning the perishable from the truth. From then on, you experience glory, victory, magnificence, beauty, abundance, Love, Light, and peace.

Sadhana is a reminder to remain vigilant, constant vigilance in words, as well as in actions and thoughts.[1] How can you raise your consciousness to dignity, to nobility, if you choose to function as a low-minded person with low values? Sadhana will take you out of gossip, and out of any activity of low vibration. Sadhana will also take you to the Invisible Being, the great Supreme Being, who lives within each of you, who guides you, and who is full of knowledge, wisdom, Love, Light, compassion, and tolerance.

Sadhana Is Not Difficult

Sadhana is not difficult. It is totally natural. What is required is to love God or your guru totally and have total faith in your mantra. If you have not been initiated into any mantra, use So Ham, use devotion, use surrender, or any practice that pleases you, and most of all, be *aware. Awareness* is the key.

Be enthusiastic and willing, and be dedicated to your sadhana. Serve everyone with Love; love with no desire or expectation. Sadhana is not hard, but natural and easy. Meditation is a natural state. Be aware and stay focused *on* your path, then little by little you dive *in* the path.

Meditation will make many things much easier. If you feel the path is difficult, know that as a result of meditation, calmness, peace, tranquility, and centeredness will arise. Until now you have meditated on mundane things, so from now on I invite you to go inside, go inward and find the treasure awaiting you. The same way you perceive the outer mundane world when your sight is turned outward, turn within and perceive the inner world, the glory of the inner world and the vastness of the inner world. Then truth starts to be consciously active in your everyday life experience. That experience then will shift from difficult to *easy*, because meditation is the natural state of your soul or your being. Only then will you move from emotional consciousness, from body consciousness, to God, to the Self, to Source consciousness.

Make time to meditate on the Self, on the Invisible Being within, the Witness within. Create a relationship with the Witness, the Self, the consciousness within. Intensify and live this relationship, cherish it, nurture it, and devote yourself to it.

Cultivate a Divine Attitude

By chanting you are nurturing your relationship with the Self. You are reminded of the Supreme who dwells within, and your heart opens. Then you start loving freely without conditions. The more you live "the awe," the more you realize your truth, your purpose on this plane. Each word you chant contains tremendous power. These words are sacred; thus, they bring Light and Love, and they purify your heart and mind.

This power will have a deep effect on you, on your whole being, and you will start experiencing the profound part of yourself. You can also be healed just by chanting, which reenergizes your cells and revitalizes your subtle bodies. These words that are chanted enter the hub of the heart, your essence is revealed, and immense joy is awakened.

Be aware. Awareness is sadhana. Sadhana is practiced to master the mind, to purify the mind. As soon as the mind is enlightened, the Higher Self reveals itself.

Cultivate the attitude of seeing Divinity in each other. When you show Love, you will receive Love. Honor others and others will definitely honor you. Bliss comes from devotion, from Love for the Supreme, because bliss is a form of Divinity and Divinity is bliss.

The Obstacles in Your Sadhana

The obstacles in your sadhana are nothing more than the ego and attachment. Those two attributes prevent you from experiencing the Principle of Higher Self, the truth, and the divine ecstasy. Give up the ego and give up all attachments and your heart will be pure again. Then naturally you'll be led to supreme wisdom.

The land of ego is fear. The fertilizer is attachment. You are so attached to this false security because you fear being alone. The entire universe is in you, so why fear being alone? Stop creating hell; hell as well as heaven is in your own hands. Don't blame God or your guru for anything. The root of all suffering is the mind. Know this: Master your mind and you will not suffer.

Honor yourself. Meditate on yourself. Go within. Your Self is pure bliss, pure consciousness. What more do you want—the ephemeral? Just know your Higher Self, and for that, drop everything else that's not necessary.

Live in the Vibration of God

When you sit with another soul, create satsang (a spiritual gathering); create the path to truth, the path to existence. Together, live in God, live in the Self and infuse the practice—the sadhana—with nobility, which will cleanse and purify the mind of its impure, unholy, non-divine tendencies (samskaras). Let your togetherness enable each of you to overcome these "negatives" of a conflicted mind.

The more you live in the vibration of God, the more divine vibrations will emanate from your being. Know that Grace will shape you; Grace will transform you on many levels, which you *may* see, as Grace works at a very subtle level, too. Be with divine company. Be in a place where your spirit gets charged in such a way that, when old samskaras appear, you have the strength to face all. Yes, you can be a realized soul through the formless or the form of God; you will reach the highest state either way.

Remember God as often as possible: dialogue, write, play, pray, chant, do japa, and read to uplift your consciousness. The name of God will take you to a state of intoxication, to bliss. Engage yourself; put God on your tongue so you are "all ways" with the awareness of the Divine. Make the practice of God an effortless moment of your daily activities. Dedicate the day to God before starting any activity, and offer every single thing or task to God, who dwells within. Obey and dedicate your actions and their results to the Supreme Intelligence, which will naturally change your attitude. That Grace will flow spontaneously. Thus humility will manifest and you will surrender.

One very important lesson is to stop identifying with your body, with roles you are given to play. To change your attitude you are also to be more aware, to stop reacting—to surrender. Allow the Shakti, the Divinity, the Christ in you to do all, and the individuality will dissolve into nothingness. Your ego will make you feel it is the doer and will deny the Divinity. However, the I AM, the Presence in you, is the doer. Increase your Love for the Source, long for the Presence, and intensify the Love in your heart for the Lord. You have the free will to think, to pray, and to love at any moment, no matter what activities you are engaged in. This is freedom that no one can take from you.

Make of God your best friend, God as the Great Mother, God as Lord. Speak all fears or problems to God and trust Her or Him fully. Silence your speech and you will silence the mind. Only then will the small "I" (the lower self), the ego, and the world disappear. Then you will meet the unknown in the depth of your being. Cultivate virtues, cultivate good company, and choose the highest.

Know that you are already realized. You have "all ways" been free, but you have simply not been aware, just as when you get up in the morning and know that what you experienced during sleep was a dream. It is not real, and in the same way, one day you'll realize, you'll awaken to, the non-reality of what was your everyday life. You are, in truth, eternally free, ever pure, totally enlightened, the liberated I AM.

10

The Sadhaka's Prayer

Today, now, I fully accept my stepping

into truth, the eternal truth.

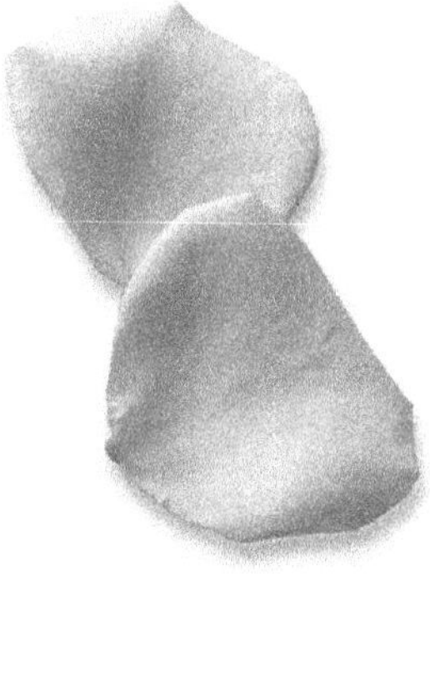

The Sadhaka's Prayer

Beloved Almighty Presence, thank you, thank you for all you constantly offer, and blessings to you, Most Precious. I call for your assistance, for intense action of the Violet Cosmic Perfection to be active in my whole being, in my akashic record, in my karma, consuming all shadows in me, releasing all human creation from my being. I ask to have myself cut from this human consciousness and its patterns and habits. Yes, help me to be "in" this world, but not "of" this world, to transmute all acceptance and memory of disease and old age with death.

From the Flame of my heart, I offer blessings to you, Elohim of the Violet Ray, for your service to all of us. Please activate your Flame in all my subtle bodies and in the organs and glands of my physical body. Activate purity and obedience to the Light within my chakras and mind and the particles of my being. With magnetic power, dissolve all human limitations within my whole being.

I ask for assistance and I choose to be the freedom that I am. Lift my vibration, lift my consciousness, and disconnect my energies from the creation of human negativities. I request all the feelings of Cosmic Action to establish Divinity within me and my world, to teach me how to vibrate with your divine consciousness, to activate the law of resonance in me, to make me feel the Cosmic Action within, to take me to a higher state of consciousness during the resting time of this body, and to activate the law of forgiveness. Yes, Beloved Almighty Presence, I choose the path of Light in its glory, living fully in the victory of Love.

Dearest Archangels, so many times you have offered assistance that I have refused. Today, now, I fully accept my stepping into truth, the eternal truth. Purify my whole being with the vibration and Presence of truth.[1]

Sai Maa with the children of Bet Lar, India, a remote village in the foothills of the Himalayas.

11

Align with Your Supreme Self

Center yourself in the
vibration of the Godself within
and just say "yes" to the Light.

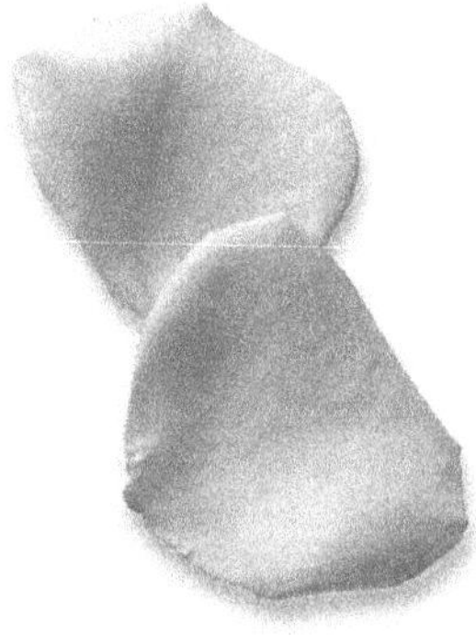

Align with Your Supreme Self

Choose to Realize the Presence Within

You are a spirit in a physical body. Remember when anyone says anything false about you, you are just to love him or her. Remember, too, even when you are good to people, you may be accused of selfish motives; do good anyway. If you're successful, you will win false friends and enemies; succeed anyway. Always remember that whatever good you do today will be forgotten tomorrow; do good anyway. Honesty and sincerity make you vulnerable. Be honest. Be frank anyway. That is your power, your strength with yourself. Those who come to you and need your help—a few minutes later they may attack you. Help them anyway and anyone else.

Be happy. Be happy. Even better, make everyone happy.

Give the world the best of you—the *best* of you!

I received this question in the mail: "What kind of initiation do I need to experience my I AM Presence?" The consciousness of I AM is God. It is your Godself, your Godhood, and there is no need of an initiation. You are to choose the highest of your personality and move into that I AM Consciousness, that I AM Purity. From incarnation to incarnation, you've been seeking this unification of consciousness and personality, calling it the true Self, calling it the Divine, the Supreme, the Source, the universe. All religions are taking you to the same space, and that space is within you.

To experience the I AM Principle, you must go deep inside and be in joy. *The only energy that takes you to the I AM is joy,* and to experience that energy is your choice. If you choose not to experience the I AM Principle within, you become the victim of your personality. You must choose to move into that space where you expand with the breath of the Divine within. I do encourage each of you to discover your true Self and avoid getting caught in any initiation or ritual. Still, rituals are excellent for washing and clarifying the mind. When they are performed there is no time for you to think.

Again, you are to feel the "breath" of your embodiment of the Christ Principle within. There is nothing greater than this breath. You incarnated to enjoy and to bless everything you experience on this earth, and to bless all with Love and illumination. Being your own person in your own Light, collaborate and contribute to the uplifting of the consciousness of mankind. Feel the "one breath" of life, focus with joy on this breath, and identify with the true being who you are, the I AM Presence, the Christ. Then the Divine Mother will carry out every divine desire and wish, because this is how She loves you. She will prepare you for the Christ Consciousness and to receive everything you wish.

Choosing every *thought,* every *word*, and every *breath* is higher than any ritual. Do not expect an initiation to take you to self-realization. Allow your choices to come directly from the I AM. Imagine that each feeling, each word is a blessing for humanity and for the planet. You now are in the conscious awareness of your I AM Presence, your heart, and your head. Allow your words to vibrate with the Holy breath of the I AM. Be in joy and connect with your

Self in the manifestation of the Divine. You are to remember that you are the Creator, to respect every decision, every word that you say.

You are vibrating to the frequency of your magnificent Mother Earth in her awakening, and you are to bring this magnificent Light into yourself. Caring for yourself is caring for her and caring for all. You are your own being—growing, expanding or contracting, depending on your choices. Stand in your truth. You know exactly what your truth is, and you know exactly when you are standing in your truth. This is the creative energy, the Presence of God within, the Supreme Divine Intelligence. Move with it, play with it, and discover yourself as a divine being. Be a child, be with this Presence and walk with it. This Infinite Intelligence will take you everywhere.

Give to your breath the divine sound, and do not use your words lightly. All of you are masters of the Light; plant the Light in your workdays and thought forms, so when you speak it is Holy breath. Allow the breath to be Holy within you. This is Christ on Earth. The flame of the divine Love within you will spring forth and shower its glory upon you as you expand to serve others. Be a vehicle of this Light; know it is very easy for you if you move with joy into your Godself.

Oh, Beloveds, this is the time of great change on this planet. Never before have so many beings been asking, "What is the sense of my life? Where am I going?" You are to use this opportunity to expand. Many have already entered this Presence and are waiting for others to join this circle of Light. This Light will come to you in your dream state or in meditation; it will come to you! This Light is yours—be in the Light and merge with the Light!

Yes, be the Light! Enter the dimension of the Divine that is prepared for you. As you read this, think of your sacred abode of the Divine, then move into it. Let your awareness shift. This is where the Godhead is. Experience your wholeness, your fullness, and your Divinity. Center yourself in the vibration of the Godself within and just say "yes" to the Light.[1]

This is the one pure moment. How precious is the "now," how divine and how expanded is the "now."[2] Be still and know that the center of your being has always existed and is here now. You are living through the living Light. Be that and allow it to happen. Do not fear.

Be deep in alignment with the Supreme Self within. Allow yourself to be taken into the Light, and in that moment you will experience peace. Be the divine child and stand in your own Light that you know is your truth. Allow the glory of this Light to expand. Be in joy. Be at peace.

Drop everything—all maya—and serve only the Highest, the Supreme. Breathe it! This is the "one breath." Breathe the Highest in all your activities. Go beyond the feeling, beyond thought. Open your heart to experience true strength. Consciously connect your personality to your Highest Self, and allow this field of Light to activate this field of energy, to activate your higher purpose. Remember that you are divine and your nature is joy. Consciously experience this in silence.

Know your intention, be your intention, be wrapped in it and know clearly you are the *creator* of your own intentions. Open yourself to your divine intention. Radiate through you the Light of the Creator. Remember God and your divine heritage. You are the One and with your Love you are to glorify this Shakti. Radiate this divine intelligence with your Light and your Love, and with your powerful intention allow the glory of the Shakti to shine through you.

Do not hesitate to call on the Shakti with your power and Love. Anchor this power of Love in the planet. Raise all your thought forms to your Godhood and be wrapped in this devotion. Nothing else is needed—no initiations.

God, God, God. Only God.

12

Seek the Clarity of Higher Consciousness

You are the reason; you are the Light

—this is the coming of the new consciousness.

Seek the Clarity of Higher Consciousness

Allow Your Personality to Be Transformed

Honor your soul's courage by fully accepting this earthly existence. This earthly existence brings many challenges and opportunities for you to move into the real purpose for your existence on this plane. Receive and feel the harmonious divine Love embracing the full spectrum of your being.

Yes, Beloveds, I know you are moving through deep changes, transformations, and shifts. Moving into the divine power allows the personality to be transformed, to be transmuted into an awakening state of consciousness. Contemplation, meditation, and awareness are what will lead you to that space of fullness.

Because of what is happening on this planet, many are asking, "Who am I?" This has not happened before. You are all here to experience the highest of yourselves, together, on all levels. I know it is not always easy to move from flesh, emotion, and mind to spirit, but know that the path of the heart is the only path to be in.

Within the body there are divine places and you are to explore them. They are situated in the chakras.[1] When you reach the heart chakra, you can experience many different states of consciousness. For instance, you can experience deep Love and, after a few minutes or seconds, you can experience anger towards the same being. A few minutes after that you can experience fear, jealousy, envy, and greed.

You are constantly shifting, and you are more aware of it when you are "in the path," *in* your sadhana. You are to remember that you are not the flesh, not the body, and that change is difficult and requires discipline. Sometimes our pain and suffering bring us to God. With this knowledge, you should not blame or judge anyone who may be going through this process, this change of consciousness. Again, remember that if you choose, desire, and seek inner balance, you must go within. Respect yourself for this choice. Dig into this inner treasure of beauty and experience for yourself the wisdom of Supreme Light and Shakti.

Stay focused with the name of God on your tongue. By being with others for meditation, for sharing and caring, we serve each other. Then we move into a higher consciousness of our being. The power of God within will serve you in a way you cannot now understand with your mind. Only through surrender to the Light, to God, and to the guru can you go beyond these worldly emotions.

The first step is your willingness to forgive others and yourself, your willingness to move into the action of divine will. This is the only way to free yourself from your emotional reactions and attitudes. This will take you into a deeper and greater clarity. Again, do not blame, because blame does not empower your exploration and personal growth. Remember, whenever you shift your belief system, your I AM Presence and your soul will have energy immediately for you. Then your spirit nature, your soul, will have more influence on your everyday life.

There is inside each of you many levels of divine energy, and you are to accept guidance from there. You are not a human being; you are a spirit in human form. You are to remember that you are divine and move from this grossness, this physical matter, to the Divine. As you do this, you experience a shift of energy that causes pain, because you are not used to this other divine level of energy. When anger, guilt, fear, and challenges appear, it is only through the divine Love within that these emotions will shift. This is what you call the shadow, the ego, and the darkness. You may *choose* to shift—you hold the key in your hands. Your life is in your hands. Surrender to God and bring that chaos into the Light.

When your thoughts and emotions become more loving, there is joy that you cannot describe with words. When you demonstrate to yourself and to others that you love and care for one another, this is worshipping God. This is the nature of your own heart.

When you can, be by yourself, sit or lie down and reflect on your personality. Reflect on how much you care for others. Divine Love can never leave you. It doesn't matter how people treat you. What matters is to continue expressing your Love and wisdom. Show compassion for the struggles of humanity. Allow forgiveness to come into your mind, your thought forms, and your heart. Only then can you forget the past and bring yourself to the "now" moment, into the present, not the past and not the future. Your manifesting ability is enhanced by the release of your negative thoughts, so surrender to Love and forgive all persons, places, and things in your life that have hurt you.

We have been through many changes together, all of us, and we are to remember the Love that brought us together. So often we forget the Love and we forget the gratitude. We forget to be grateful. Whether it is money or work, they will never replace Love. In the past it was the money, the work and not the relationship; now it's about the Love, about the relationship of caring. It's about being alive and remembering with each breath that God is within you.

I know that you are a child of God. I know you are a bright Light, capable of bringing the divine Light and peace into this world. Also remember many are supporting the work you are doing here. You are the reason; you are the Light—this is the coming of the new consciousness. Feel this power right now, above you, around you and on all sides. Feel it in front of you. It is right here for you. The universe is shifting, as you are shifting. As you love it, it loves you. Life is always smiling at you, and this smile is your potential.

Mother Earth is giving, so giving. Be like her and be one with all nature. Look at a tree, how much it gives to the moment, how nature never stops giving. Forget everything that does not serve you anymore. Feel the beauty of God's glory and know that the soul wants to express itself. If you stay in the personality, the soul cannot express itself.

There is nothing else but God. Nothing!

13

What Is Your Choice?

You are created in the image of God,
so reach within yourself to this consciousness.
Ask yourself, "What are my true desires?
What am I choosing?"

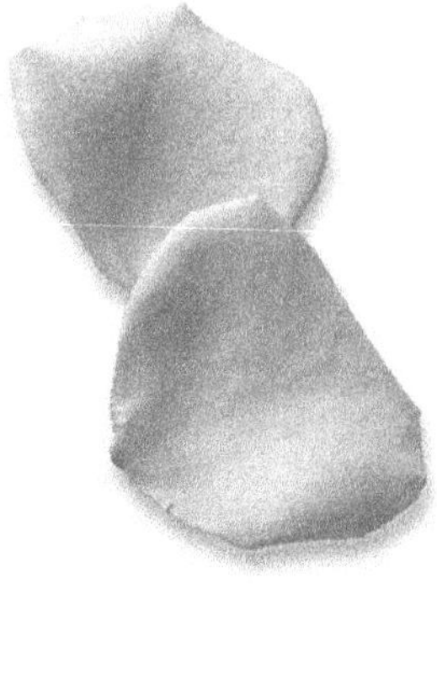

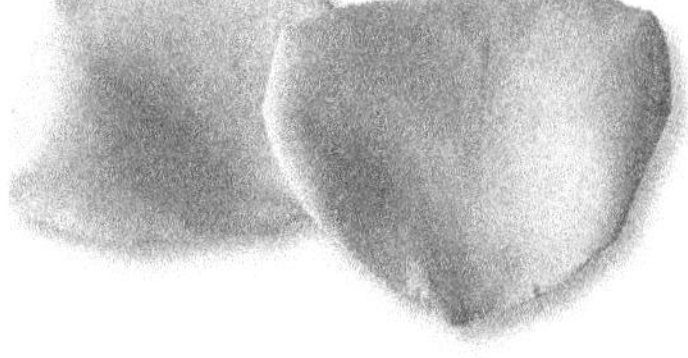

What Is Your Choice?

We Live in Fear or in Love

Every heart is the abode of God, and every heart blazes in and with divine Light. Even if you are unaware of the Presence, the Presence is there. Every being is yearning for happiness and freedom. Everyone is engaged, in one way or another, in finding Love.

This divine Love is your birthright, and you *can* reach this state; trust yourself. Joy is your nature. Tap into it. Peace is your nature. Be it. Love is your essence. Choose to experience it. Expansion is the "real you." Again, choose it. When I say, "All is possible," know that all *is* possible. You are created in the image of God, so reach within yourself to this consciousness. Ask yourself, "What are my *true* desires? What am I *choosing*?" I emphasize again that all is within you. With your sadhana, start to experience within you the tangible Presence of joy, peace, and Love.

Through sadhana you can move from limitation to vastness, to infinity, to divine consciousness. *Know sadhana is not hard.* There is an infinite Source within you. You are the truth—the "changeless" is in you. When you move beyond the worldly and the perishable, you live in absolute freedom.

You are blessings of Grace; you are in the path of Grace. This Grace transcends every energy that is not valid anymore until you become the Transcendent itself. The limited consciousness shifts, and you live in the Grace of expanded consciousness. When the body-sense consciousness is transcended, you are free.

You know that the guru's Grace, the divine Grace, the Grace of your I AM, supports you fully. All of you are embodiments of Grace because Grace is an attribute of truth. There is only one divine consciousness. Within each of you there is an exquisite joy, divine joy, perfect joy, and in doing sadhana, sometimes with your awareness you start tapping into that joy. The guru always pours a tremendous amount of Grace into the deserving disciple.

The core of your being is full of Grace. Go inward and experience it. Do not wait. Do not doubt. Doubt is the enemy of your sadhana. This joy will not be given to you by an outsider, by a friend, or a spouse. It comes only from you. Those who live in Maha Bhakti can share with you their joy, the joy that uplifts and elevates you, the joy that purifies the mind and the heart.

You Can Change Your Life, Yourself

If any one of you has expectations, just drop them. An "alarm" is going off in the world—an alarm telling you to feel compassion for each other, to love each other. Mankind is longing to be loved. Humanity is yearning to be loved, this Love where there are no conditions, where no matter what happens you know you are loved.

We are all created from the same Love, the same pure space. And because you have come out of alignment, you have forgotten who your Self is, your inner Self. Whatever you see happening in the world, know that it is a reflection of each of you. Individually you are all struggling inside, in a state of war.

The only path to unity with yourself, to harmony within yourself, is in the moment when you fully accept yourself and stop judging yourself and others. The more you judge yourself, the more you will judge others. The more you judge others, the more you will judge yourself. There is such power within you, such Grace, such Love within your being, such Light and glory.

The glory of God is within all religions and not one is bad. Are you "full" enough within yourself to accept another religion? Are you ready to fully embrace the Self so you can embrace others? Everyone is longing to be accepted and loved.

In this context, you should know why you are seeing more and more disease on the planet—more and more. These diseases exist simply because your subtle bodies are not in harmony. Because your energy is not in harmony, your physical bodies cannot be harmonious, and that is because you feel you are not loved. I can love you at this very moment, this moment of Glory, this blessed moment. I *am* loving you, although you may not feel loved, which is a different subject.

We all live in fear or in Love. When you live in fear you contract your cells, your DNA. You contract everything within you. But when you live in Love, you expand. The choice is in your hands.

For those already on a spiritual path or *in* a spiritual path, it's important to understand that you can transform your own karma.[1] You can change your life, yourself. Do not rely on someone else. Do not expect someone else to choose these things for you. You were put on this planet, in this civilization, for a reason. On this plane of free will, if you do not choose for yourself, no one is going to choose for you.

14

The Eternal Nature of the Self

Self is truth, wisdom and knowledge,

boundless and free, beyond space and time.

The Self illuminates everything.

The Eternal Nature of the Self

Universal Consciousness Waits to Be Discovered

Death is the one common or usual fact of human existence, yet instead of preparing yourselves to face that moment, most of you choose to ignore it, to avoid thinking about it. Some even refuse to hear about death. Without exception, all of you are to confront the mortality of your and your beloveds' physical bodies. Most think it's the end of life; it may be the end of physicality, but it definitely is not the end of consciousness. Death has not yet been integrated into your experience of life, as knowledge of life and wisdom of life.

Death does not exist. Your being is beyond the experience of birth or "death"–you are eternal. The fear of death occurs because of a lack of knowledge and because of ignorance. Most of you see existence as identification with the body, which is falsehood. You are playing a role; you are changing a costume–that's what your body is. It's a play of consciousness. All fear vanishes when you live in the knowingness of who you are, your *true* identity.

There is within you a free consciousness waiting to be discovered.[1] Introspection helps you to understand that you live in a world of falsehood. Only by coming out of the ignorance of falsehood and duality do you experience the true knowledge. When you know who you are, you realize the body can be destroyed, can be killed, but never the Eternal in you, which is pure consciousness and indestructible, with no birth or death. This is the immortal part of yourself, your soul. Introspection, silence, meditation, sadhana, and spiritual practice will free you from the most deep fear-based expression of this falsehood and take you to the non-death experience of life.

Those of you who can "see" death can use this ability for your sadhana—see the body disintegrating, lying in a cemetery, becoming dust or being burnt. A person may have been very, very wealthy, very selfish. Death has taken the wealth from him or her, because when you leave the planet, all matter stays here. To be with God, you are alone.

Many fear to be with God, to meet God, but the death experience can be very peaceful, like when you go to sleep and are totally at ease. Imagine that you go to sleep for hundreds of nights and one day wake up in a different form. It can be a beautiful experience only when no fear is present.

Be happy for someone who leaves the physical envelope. It's Love, it's freedom, freedom from duality, pain, pleasure, good, or bad. The Self, the soul, the Higher Self, is not dying. It is possible for you to leave this plane peacefully by chanting the divine name of God, by reading the scriptures, or by evoking a Holy moment.

This is how the death experience will be. When you practice good actions, you can die peacefully. Wealth, good positions, husbands, wives, and possessions do not mean anything at the moment of death, no matter how much you have. All leave this world without material possessions. Worldly wealth has no meaning at that moment; only *inner* wealth has meaning. Divine wealth takes you to the Divine. Depending upon how you spent your life, you will experience only one of two paths: One is Light, beauty, joy, contentment, and merging with Divinity. The other is non-light, based in fear.

The body is a field where whatever you sow, you reap. You will reap the consequences of your actions. Prepare yourself well for the final physical journey. If you choose deliverance and freedom, be vigilant, always devoted to God and to Love.

All Illness Is Falsehood

Know that I have no advice to give for beings with illnesses such as cancer. What I *can* say is that when physical dis-ease or physical dis-orders come, you are to face them with courage, calmness, faith, and Love, knowing that all diseases are related to fear, to falsehood and non-truth. The cells are Light in origin, and Light is truth, so they must shift back into divine Light and Grace. Your cells are not meant for death or disease, but for Light and delightful experiences.

Remember, for the body the highest victory is perfect health. Receive strength from your I AM Presence, which means full divine power in all your subtle bodies. The stronger they are, the healthier they are. Then the subtle bodies will refuse sickness, refuse the force of disease. Before you can feel or see any disorders in your physical body, they are in the subtle bodies. Healing is created by working with your cells with faith in the Light, returning truth and supreme harmony to those cells. *All* disease is falsehood. *All* illness is falsehood.

What about contemplating your art of living? What are your expectations in that domain? There is such power within you. Trust this power. It is God Himself. Do you take time for quiet moments or are you always "busy"? Are you willing to fully experience the Divine within you?

Again remember, every illness is falsehood.[2] It is not a natural state for the physical. Feel the faith within you and use it. Also, contemplate the message your body is sending. What is the universe telling you?

The Self Exists as Peace and Joy

How can I talk of the Self? The nature of Self is so mysterious, so subtle, the subtlest of the whole universe. The Self is form and the Self is formless; nameless, yet it is given names. Self is pure consciousness, is life force and bliss, omnipotent and omnipresent. Self is truth, wisdom and knowledge, boundless and free, beyond space and time. The Self illuminates everything. It's strange to speak of the unspeakable. The Self is to be experienced as the most powerful message of God. The Self is beyond anything you experience with words.

This bliss of the Higher Self is always new. The laughter of the Self is completely different from the pleasure of the senses. You know, those of you who depend on the senses for your everyday happiness, how you search for this happiness from one object or place to another, new things, new this, new that, just for the sake of satisfaction. But with the Self, you have "new" by itself. The Self is in you, in its highest, in its fullness. The Self is the foundation of your life experience. It is peace, joy, Love, and truth. It reveals itself by the Grace of the guru, by the Grace of the Self.

When you are being "purified," the Self appears. It can be anywhere, any time, in any situation, even when you are tired or in a crisis. The Self is Light. The Self is silence. The Self is the All. The Self is the Witness. The Self is the observer. The Self *supports* all but does not become involved, is unattached. The Self *experiences* all and is still unattached. The Self is victory. The Self is glory. There is "no thing" greater than the Self . . . *and you are the Self!*

15

What Is Enlightenment?

When you understand that you are only consciousness,
there is "no thing" to do, no liberation to seek,
no ignorance to come out of, no karma, no personal
or individual responsibility, "no thing" to become.
Just be and it unfolds by itself.

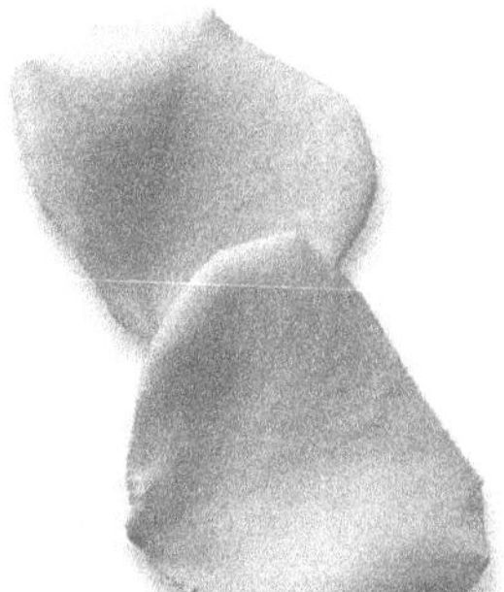

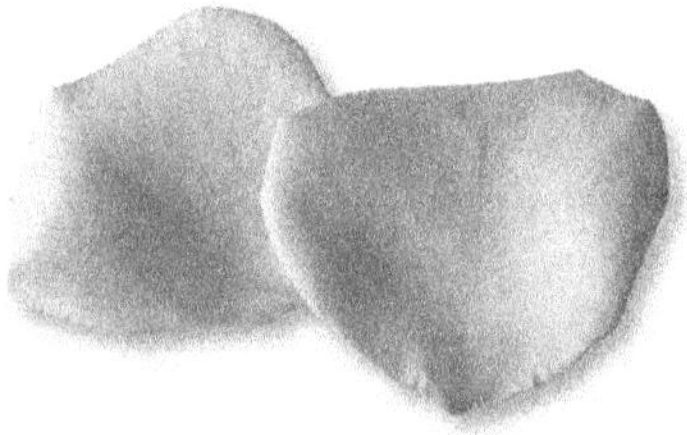

What Is Enlightenment?

Reason and Logic No Longer Have Meaning

Enlightenment is so simple that it cannot easily be explained by words. It is like a state of freedom in which social rules, self-image, or ideals do not exist anymore. In simple words, you no longer care what others think about you. It is freedom with no fear whatsoever. To *be* in that state, you must realize you are not the body but are the Higher Self, who is in charge of making the body function. You are the Higher Self, the consciousness watching, completely free and not limited by body, mind, or senses.

I assume that now you understand about attachment to "bodies" or "objects." As soon as identification with the body is over, you are free; then you can *be* consciousness itself, everywhere and in everything. Then the *real* is! You are the Light, the Love, the truth, the God, and the Source. All is consciousness. When you are thinking as the individual, there's duality. As long as you live in *that* state of consciousness, liberation is impossible. Oneness is impossible. If you have faith in these words or in me, you will understand without being in conflict with yourself. Also know that it is only the lower self who is in conflict, in doubt, in duality or confusion—the Higher Self, *never*.

Enlightenment has nothing to do with the logic you develop in school, has nothing to do with the mental body. No longer will reason and logic have meaning. Live in faith. This faith will bring more power from your inner being. Faith is necessary in sadhana, because you will experience a state while in your body that cannot be explained in words—*Unity*.

So many times I say, "Drop even the desire for enlightenment because this desire is a great obstacle." It's like a screen between your soul and you, between *You* and you. For enlightenment, joy and truth in feelings are necessary, are a must. Know that when refusing to forgive, you carry a burden, which is bondage and non-freedom. Without forgiving, you cannot be in the joy needed for liberation. That is why you are to be happy with yourself. It is a first step toward joy. If you cannot forgive, it's because you are holding onto a desire. Desire prevents you from experiencing the reality of the Higher Self, the truth of life and of feelings.

When you have difficulty forgiving, it means that inside you there is judgment and conflict, right and wrong. Because of ignorance, you judge and can't forgive. Remember, you create your own world, your conflict and confusion, from concepts or ideas created by the mind, by lack of sincerity or lack of truth. Ignorance is a concept created by the mind of man.

Your mind is dualistic and keeps you separated from the truth of who you are. How can you trust this mind? For example, it's strange for me to say "I love you," because "I" and "you" suggest that there are two, whereas there is only the *One, one Self*. It is the same Self in you that is in me. There is only the One.[1]

As I explain during workshops, you are not the doer. You are actually "nothing." When you know you are consciousness, then you are only a witness. By being a witness, you are free, liberated. Dance with the Divinity within, the divine splendor.

Now, where does this sense of ignorance come from? It's simple: It comes from the fact that you think you are the body or the mind or the senses. So why are you attached to the body? Simply because there is no Love. There is only attachment, which is bondage. Love is freedom.

You can create something, let's say harmony, but you cannot create the *true feeling of Love*, because such soul-to-soul interaction is outside your mind's domain. There is no lasting truth in ideas, in intellectual creation. Ask yourself how many minutes your ideas last and you'll know if they are changeless. Then realize that you are divine *truth*.

Anchor the Truth of Your I AM

What is it that keeps a person from speaking his or her truth, his or her feelings? Ask yourself this question: "How can I be in a healthy relationship with myself if I am not sincere or true with myself?" It also would be impossible to be in a healthy relationship with another.

When lying to yourself, naturally the law of life will create discomfort, contraction, confusion, and manipulation. The same law of life (how much Shakti Jesus put into the word "life") will also create comfort and inner freedom when you live *with* and *in* the current of its expansion, its joy. Then the feeling of "I AM That Inner Self" finally exists in your everyday life, experiencing itself as fullness.

When you move step-by-step into enlightenment, there will come a point when you will be nearly ninety percent out of fear, and the remaining ten percent of your experience will be strong fear, even *very* strong fear. This is because your ego is so scared of its death that the personality creates a completely "new" but familiar pattern to again reassure you with false security. This is another way, a disguised way, of denying yourself.

Your ego knows what to bring to you, to make you shift your focus, to move you from freedom to non-freedom, to shift your boundaries. The ego has been so brilliant for so long. You have given it power so it is powerful and controls you. It will take you to see, live, and experience its way; and you will trap yourself again in the same old pattern, as you always have.

A being who was sick was taking antibiotics and felt it was better to stop the pills after three days instead of taking the whole treatment, and his condition worsened. I explained to him that all the bacteria were not dissolved and that the strongest ones had survived. They were *victorious*. The same truth applies to the *ego* and the *personality*.

Baba says that no one comes to him to ask for truth, only for reasons of bondage, bondage which comes from attachments, belief systems, and identification with the lower self. You see, a real guru is concerned about the pain and suffering of his or her students and is *"all ways"* ready to wash from each their worldly conditions. This is *Love*. All gurus know that every being is the *Higher Self*, even though each keeps identifying with ego-mind-personality or with the body. The guru only sees the Light, the beauty, and the consciousness, rather than the human creation imprisoned by rationality, by embracing belief systems, ideas, ideals, reason, and so forth. Of course, society also has a great influence on your personality and your self-image.

To live a Godly life, a totally divine life, no self-image created by the mind and by society can exist. The way you will view life will no longer be social; it will be the way Divinity sees, a life free from ignorance, free from illusion. It will be knowledge, knowingness, truth, and the Light. *Enlightening.*

Desires which create judgments bind you. When judging others, you are judging yourself. How can you experience liberation if you are judging? It is impossible. The mind to which you are giving power is creating its own world, with fear. As soon as the mind feels threatened, all its "right" and "wrong" start. Judgments arise. In these judgments, what is the mind doing? Defending itself, justifying itself, practicing self-justification, self-defense, giving rational reasons to "feel" good about thinking the "right" thing, about using rational ideas or concepts to "feel" happy.

The mind gives power to the head over the heart, disconnecting you from true, real feelings. Your soul speaks the truth to you, but the mind separates you from your Higher Self because of fear. Fear is guiding your experience of life. If you wish to live in the fullness of the Higher Self, then feelings of truth and the gift of the "now," the present moment, have to be in your life. The "now" has no beginning and no end and is "all ways" eternal. In the fullness of the moment there is no fear; whereas, when you start judging others or yourself, you stop the flow of expansion.

So there is a natural contraction, a discomfort, a non-free state in which you can hurt yourself. It is easy to rationalize when you choose denial, which also creates judgments. From judging, your manipulation starts, all based on fear. This is because the mind has the need to protect itself—duality, the dual mind versus the heart. How many years have you wondered, "What's wrong?" In the meantime years are passing and you have not found yourself.

To be free, you have to be courageous. Your soul knows exactly what to put in your path for you to grow, mature, and *be*. To *be* yourself, be free, be expanded—be yourself and listen to your Higher Self. Even if you feel like a beginner and have read these lines again and again, there will be a "click" at a certain moment and you will become enlightened.

Truth, therefore, is to be listened to over and over again. How many things do you do over and over again? So practice truth again and again until you understand. Refine your intellect so that the Self easily shines through. *Re*read, *re*hear. These repetitions are part of the rituals of life.

For instance, I watch the sun rise. There is never the same energy, though it looks the same—again, repetition. Truth. Truth can be experienced in a fraction of a second. That truth is this: You are absolute perfection, limitless, infinite, with all and every quality of the Creator and the Creation.

So when the intellect is clear, enlightenment occurs, because no obstruction is stopping the brightness, the illumination. Nothing is blocking this Divinity, this divine Light, from shining, from expressing its freedom and itself through your intellect, senses, and body. How do you clear the path for the Supreme One? How do you clear the way? By "good" and "positive" thoughts and actions. This is the way to "de-create" in your own field of energy everything you've created that is or was destroying you.

For enlightenment, discipline is needed. No practice is needed. It's an instant occurrence. There is no need for a path of spirituality, no need for a goal. You are to drop all the ideas you have created about enlightenment. They are *ideas*. I received a fax asking my advice on fasting to experience enlightenment.

Fast in the mind. If I consider myself a teacher, I would say my teaching does not require fasting. This teaching is so simple that there is no teaching, only remembering. Naturally your body is lighter, your intellect lighter when you eat less, especially in the western world where you eat too much.

When you understand that you are only consciousness, there is "no thing" to do, no liberation to seek, no ignorance to come out of, no karma, no personal or individual responsibility, "no thing" to become. Just *be* and it unfolds by itself. I write "unfolds" so that you understand. Still, I am telling you everything is already unfolded. What is the one thing preventing this understanding, whose essence is also consciousness? It is the *mind*. Teach, train, and remind the mind it is consciousness and it is done.

Where is the center of your being? There is a center in everything and everywhere, so where is the *center* of your being? As soon as you find the center, bring your mind there, bring your senses there. The very instant that you are this center, you are the All, and every sense of personal matter disappears. "No thing" is yours nor belongs to you any more and you realize the All is *within you.*

16

When You Surrender to God

There is no place in the whole universe

where God's Love is not manifest,

and you are to experience that divine nectar.

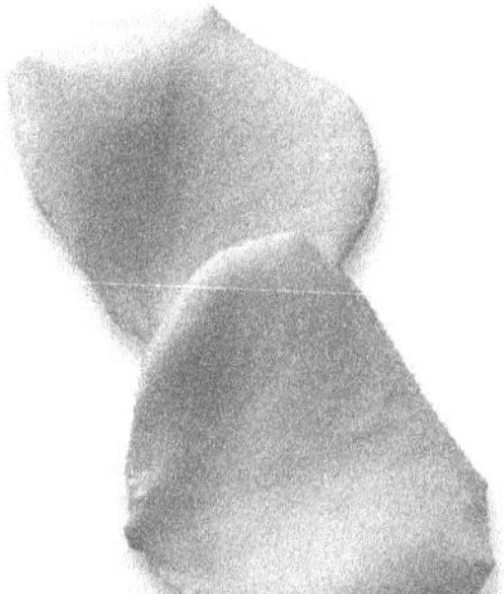

When You Surrender to God

Allow Your Heart to Open

In the lotus of your heart, God has put the treasure of the universe. Aspire to that knowledge with deep Love, long for that Divinity, and be willing with faith to enter God's abode. Divine Light is burning there for you to experience. To merge with that Light, call for Grace, yearn for Grace and for Love. Devote everything to that Grace, which will draw each of you to divine Love.

You are from God. You chose separateness for the sake of experience, and now the heart is restless, so ask for the Grace to rest in the Divine again. Only in divine Love will you find peace, joy, and bliss. Have total faith that God is the indweller within you.

Commit yourself to be in Love with God. Let your heart be open to supreme devotion. Humbly ask for Grace, humbly offer your being to God and be the lover of God. To be a disciple you must experience discipline, which will transmute the senses and clear the mind. From there your heart will open even more.

As soon as your heart opens, the path of God realization offers itself to you. Your reactions will shift to the Divine as you start mastering the senses. Fullness of devotion is in the heart. Just allow your heart to open. Devotion. Devote everything and offer your whole being to the Divine with deep devotion. The highest gift to God is devotion.

The victory and the glory of devotion never run dry. You are loved by God so immensely. God never lacks; God always gives. Allow this devotion from the sacred temple of your heart to move through every cell, allowing your whole body to be a temple. Living with pure thoughts and living in purity increases devotion. The relationship with the Supreme is experienced when your tears of Grace open your heart, a constant liberation, moving from duality to non-duality.

Surely we are blessed to be on this planet at this time, so together in Unity let us experience this blessed, radiant life in its highest. This is the glory of God's Creation. It is all Shakti. God has created devotion for us, so let us offer that devotion to God. When the Grace of your heart and the Grace of the Lord merge, you experience Divinity. Devotion is the royal path to the Divine and also the easiest. Through your devotion, the divine power that lies within you is revealed. This is the treasure of the Divine.

See God everywhere—taste God, smell God, touch God. These are to be your experiences. Divine Love never changes. It is divine and that is it. Love is a whole experience by itself.

Yearn for this devotion, yearn for this Love and I promise you, you'll experience it. Ignorance will depart, will be transmuted, and your cells will respond to that yearning. Cry for the divine Presence within, for the Christ Consciousness and the pure immaculate Love within. Create this relationship with God. Be divine, be a lover, and give every breath to the Divine.

Your true essence and the fruit of this action are beyond your expectations. As soon as you practice this consciousness of life, every moment will radiate Love, will radiate Light. The personality then will be less and less present. Your guru will see and feel your changes, the shift of your consciousness, and will be very grateful.

To experience divine Love, allow your heart to open, and offer this heart in its fullness to the Divine. Do not hold back anything. Surrender, surrender—the immortal law of the Divine is Love, so commit yourself to that law, to that purity, and that glory.

Embracing life in its fullness is devotion and is a sharing in the present moment, in the precious "now." There is no place in the whole universe where God's Love is not manifest, and you are to experience that divine nectar. In the beginning you may feel that God belongs only to you. It's okay. Merge with it and surrender.

Then you will experience Love as never before. It's a blessing to experience a pure heart. It's the divine Grace and it's the fruit of sadhana. See yourself in others and saturate your heart with Love so others can be blessed by your divine Love. The beauty of divine Love is that it grows and grows. Bliss is experienced for no reason. The fullness of your being is experienced, your Godhead is coming forth, and you are not doing anything. You are just "being"—and then you will act and speak divine truth.

All this is God experiencing God. Again, to experience ecstasy, Love, Light, and Divinity, your heart must be simple and pure, so God can bestow Grace. A pure heart is a humble heart; it is a heart devoted to God, only to God.

Loving God is loving all living creatures. God is manifesting God through all. God as the Creator manifests Himself or Herself as the Creation, so if we love God, we love God's Creation. Love is magic. God is magic. The heart is magic. Together let us serve all, serve our highest purpose. Serving all is our highest puja (ceremonial worship), our highest worship. Some people worship statues and treat humans dreadfully. Where is the Love in that? You are the living Christ, the living God, *humanity*.

Your sacred heart is full of Light, and this Light will take care of you. Allow and bring this Light into your whole body, into the conscious mind, the subconscious, and the unconscious. Surrender to this Light, to this divine consciousness, to this divine joy and divine peace, to the victory of Love and the glory of life.

Through this Love you'll experience the fullness of life. Listening to a bird sing in its fullness is God. How blessed we are. Offering yourself to God allows you to experience the fullness of God. Love is a supreme vibration, a supreme energy. Love of the Divine contains all power and all virtue.

God is Love: Love is God. The Grace of God is being poured into you. God is available to all of you, and God's Love is *for* all of you. Are you willing to experience it? What is your choice? To what do you commit yourself, and what are the benefits of a dualistic life? Consider what this worldly life is giving you. Who *are* you and what are you here for?

Beloveds, know that to experience divine Love, there are no shortcuts. Surrender, devotion, Love—these are the keys, nothing else. All is in the heart. God is your closest lover, never saying good-bye, but always here and ready for you, giving you the highest. Please go deep inside. Feel and realize that God is inside you, waiting for you to accept the divine Grace. Your essence is divine. Your essence is kindness. Love allows your mind to turn within so you can experience—in the silence of your heart—your own divine Light.

17

The Glory of Seva

Make every place you go, a place of Love, a place of service. This is selfless service, seva, a place of bhakti, and a place of transformation.

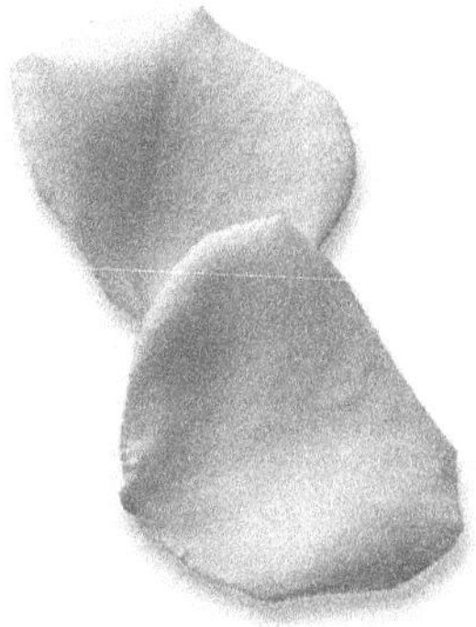

The Glory of Seva

Manifest Your True Purpose

This is a golden opportunity to serve your soul, to feel your soul, and to serve yourself so you will serve others even better. The experience of seva is the experience of your Divinity. It's a journey from your self to your Higher Self. It's a vital contribution to your incarnation on this plane.

Seva is service, service in action, Grace in action. Seva is knowledge in action, is service in devotion and will in action. Evoked for the highest purpose, it is worship. Seva is chanting the divine name; seva is pleasing the Lord within each; seva is Grace; seva is meditation; seva is the glory of the Supreme Lord of your own essence. Seva, when practiced with Love, enthusiasm, joy, and no expectations, becomes the deepest spiritual practice. As you allow the radiance of Grace and Love to shine forth in every action, you are manifesting your purpose.

When seva is practiced, Love is put into practice with no expectations. Offer your heart and your service selflessly. Seva is a spiritual practice, and this aspect will remind you to keep your heart open and your mind focused on your purpose in life. All of these are only tools to support your living in Love, in Divinity, and in seeing Divinity in each other. This gift to yourself can be the greatest treasure of your practice.

Live with total faith in your Higher Self, total faith in truth and in God. *You are That.* Experience this greatness *within yourself.*

During this journey toward inner perfection, you are to carefully, delicately approach your mind, because your purpose is to master it. Since God is at the source of the mind, dive into your practice and experience your own transformation. Embrace your Self. Experience your radiant inner Light, the God within. This gift of inner awakening and spiritual unfolding, this inner awareness and Grace, will lead a seeker to be a finder. This Grace is the essence of "remembrance." Knowledge, understanding, experience, surrender, and devotion are sacred elements of spiritual growth and unfolding.

Wherever you go, spiritual power and Love will exist. Whatever you experience will lead you to know your supreme heart, where the Lord and the Shakti dwell, where the Divinity constantly reveals itself to you.

This is an opportunity to refresh your heart and to reach a profound state of meditation, to consciously expand inner wisdom and serve your purpose in life, and to love.

Seva Is Service to God

How devoted nature is to us. The sky is a magnificent purple and pink. Every season has its own glory as it magically unfolds its own treasures. With deep devotion, nature offers such a humble example in this rendezvous of beauty and selfless service. This is the power of Love and the power of welcoming again and again in divine Grace.

When you love all that you do, transformation is guaranteed. Go ahead, *go ahead* and experience. Make every place you go, a place of Love, a place of service. This is selfless service, seva, a place of bhakti, and a place of transformation.

These practices are the source of joy and bliss. From these, life reveals its glory to each of you and inner transformation takes place. Every breath is designed to take you to the highest potential of your own being. Welcoming fully each moment is welcoming God, welcoming the Divine.

Real welcoming allows the goodness of another being to be released, to bring out the Love in their heart and allow their Light to shine. Know that when you are busy supporting others, God is busy helping and supporting you. Seva, selfless service, is service to God. Purity of heart in seva is very dear to the Supreme, just as a pure offering with no desire for reward is also very dear to the Supreme.

The sole purpose of service is to fulfill your longing to merge with and into the truth. Very, very often when the guru gives you seva, your samskaras are transmuted and karma is washed. Seva is the fruit of the guru. Where Love and seva are a path to the inner world of divine Love, Grace rushes into your sacred heart, the abode of God. So when you serve with purity of devotion, you are close to God or the guru. Then you live fearlessly and continuous showers of Grace, as an ocean without tides, pour into you.

18

Be Peace

If we all were to choose peace,

then we would quickly bring this planet,

this exquisite planet, into peace.

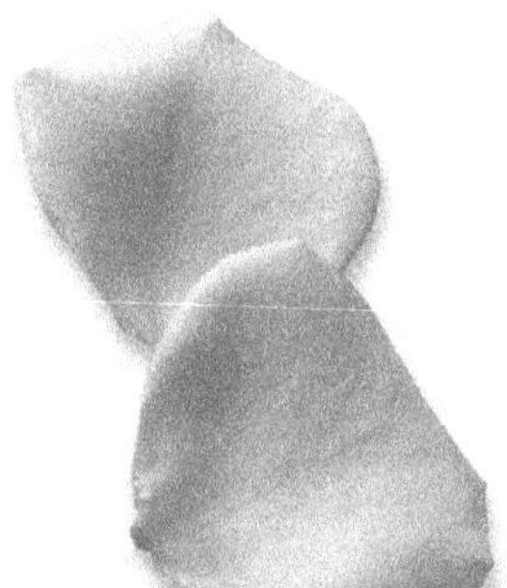

Be Peace

Stillness Allows Peace to Reveal Itself

All carry peace. Peace is the Self and the All is the Self, so the All is peace. Practice peace, sadhana of peace, the spiritual practice of peace. Supreme peace is your birthright. You inherited peace from the Higher Self, so peace is in you.

This morning one of my beloveds said, "It's so peaceful here today." Awareness—when there is Love, there is peace. Most go to a church, to a mosque, to a mandir (a temple), to darshan or to meditate in order to experience peace. Peace is an attribute of Love. It spontaneously rises from your sacred heart and embodies your whole being. Then effortlessly it spreads by itself.

Others can surely experience the peace that you are. Peace lies within your heart so do not look for it somewhere else. You may feel peaceful while in a peaceful environment, but it does not last. Inner peace, however, is yours and cannot be taken away, and this inner peace transmutes guilt, unworthiness, and more. That state of peace is within you, and *no one* besides you will create it for you—it is from inside. When there is Love for God, for the Source, you can experience peace in every moment. Peace is the Grace of Love, the Grace of the heart.

Have you noticed that after experiencing even one second of Light—your Self during meditation—you are that peace for hours or days? Your good actions will also bring from your heart to the surface the attribute of peace to flavor the personality. The more you are aware of this peace, the more you attract it. This again is Grace. This divine Grace, this inner peace, transforms your experience of life from hell to heaven. It's then your natural state.

This is how you can free yourself. In this freedom, in this peace, you will be intoxicated by divine Love. With the Love of God and the realization that you live in the being of God, you will *breathe in* the being of God. Consciously *anchor* and *expand* this energy within your conscious mind, your unconscious and your subconscious. The teaching is: *If we all were to choose peace, then we would quickly bring this planet, this exquisite planet, into peace.*

But how many people are choosing peace for the planet? How many of you, regardless of your many years of meditation, are *being* peace? Last year one of you who was in the Himalayas said, "Sai Maa, I wish I were a sadhu" (an Indian renunciant who gives up all belongings). "Well, anyone can be a sadhu," I replied. "For what reason do you wish to be a sadhu?" The answer was to live peacefully. Well, you do not have to live in the Himalayas as a sadhu to live peacefully. *Be peace* while living with your family, in your office, with your colleagues, and in society. Do not think you must live in a cave to realize God.

Peace is inside each of you, so are you ready to live the peace that you are? Are you ready to incarnate the supreme peace that you are? Are you ready? Your Higher Self carries this quality. Your Higher Self *is* that quality—tap into it. For that realization you are to move beyond duality, beyond what is perishable, beyond all judgments and resistance.

Then when you sincerely practice sadhana and discipline, you *will* experience peace. Sadhana is the seed of Divinity. As soon as you choose to know the Self, the Self will definitely reveal its divine quality of peace to you. Practice. It will come to you. Peace is the fruit of your practice.

So peace, tranquility, and serenity lie within each of you. You do not have to spend a dime to experience this inner peace—it's always in you. Be still. Be still and that stillness will allow peace to reveal itself to you.

Where does the quality of non-peace come from? It comes from the split mind, the mind of duality, of "two" and of separateness. Jealousy and greed, envy and restlessness come from the mind of duality. And your mind is then agitated.

Now, for what reason do you stay in that non-peace state? Simply because peace frightens you. It's the unknown, a state with no reference. No matter how much non-peace disturbs you, you do not choose peace. Many of you come out of a relationship of pain and suffering, of struggle and fear and you come to darshan and ask for another relationship: "Sai Maa, I do not want to be alone. Sai Maa, when will I find a partner, a soul mate?" You are so perturbed, so disturbed, due to your lack of awareness and your fear of the unknown, and you are asking for more trouble!

Beloveds, leave room for the unknown; how wondrous is the unknown; how full is the unknown; how delightful is the unknown. Peace is in you, in all of you. Peace is waiting to be your partner, your companion. You walk with peace, eat, sleep, and speak with peace, but you're not aware of its magnificent Presence, the victory of peace. Cultivate Love. Cultivate peace. Fill your being with peace, breathe peace and be aware.

At the beginning you will have to make some effort but in time it will be natural. When your guru or Higher Self sees you are making some effort, instantly Grace is bestowed. Take one step and a thousand will be taken towards you.

Explore the path, play with the path, and move in the path of peace. At any moment I can show you peace, anywhere. In that peace, you will experience the vastness of the cosmos.

So, why are you not at peace? It's lack of Love and faith. Also it's fear of surrendering and losing the fake personality—fear. Are you ready for peace? Are you humble enough to *be* peace? It happens in your daily, worldly experience of life. You will be at peace only if you choose to turn toward the peace of the Higher Self.

Ask yourself, "What are the tendencies that take me to non-peace?" During certain meditations I say, "Drop all and rest in pure consciousness." Then you are peace because this is your choice. No one can choose for you! For peace of mind, the magic recipe is to love God with your entire being—Love. The result is magic. Do not wait if you choose to *be* peace.

When you ask for peace of mind, be aware that it's right inside of you. Most of you think that non-peace and disturbances come from outside yourself. This is a mistake, because it's from your personality. You are not at peace because of your suffering, and suffering comes from desire. Desires come from your mind.

So purify your mind with good, divine thoughts by chanting and welcoming the Light into your mind. Love and Grace from your heart are waiting to serve you, *always* ready at any moment. This practice will surely expand your consciousness, your awareness, and you will live in peace and *be* peace. Only afterwards will you experience that profound silence, that serenity and tranquility.

The purity of your heart will lead you to inner peace. Stop empowering what does not serve you. The attributes of your Higher Self, your own self, and the whole universe with all its qualities, reside within you. You are so pure, so graceful, and so magnificent. Magnetize your power. Breathe the Light and the Love, and remember that Love is the greatest power. Have faith, increase your faith and live in faith.

Ascend to the highest awareness and you will then be free. The obstacles to freedom and peace are the "mine, my, myself, my-ness, I-ness" and so forth. Give up all these attachments and you will *be peace itself.* Then you will know that your essence is Love, which will fill you with peace.

I ask you for single-mindedness on God, and then you will *be* peace. Desire God, want only God, and peace will be your best companion. Feelings of humility, simplicity, innocence, Love, and compassion will be the nature of your breath. Allow Grace to intensify your Love for the I AM Presence, and you will experience supreme, divine peace.

Yes, peace is already in you, as you.

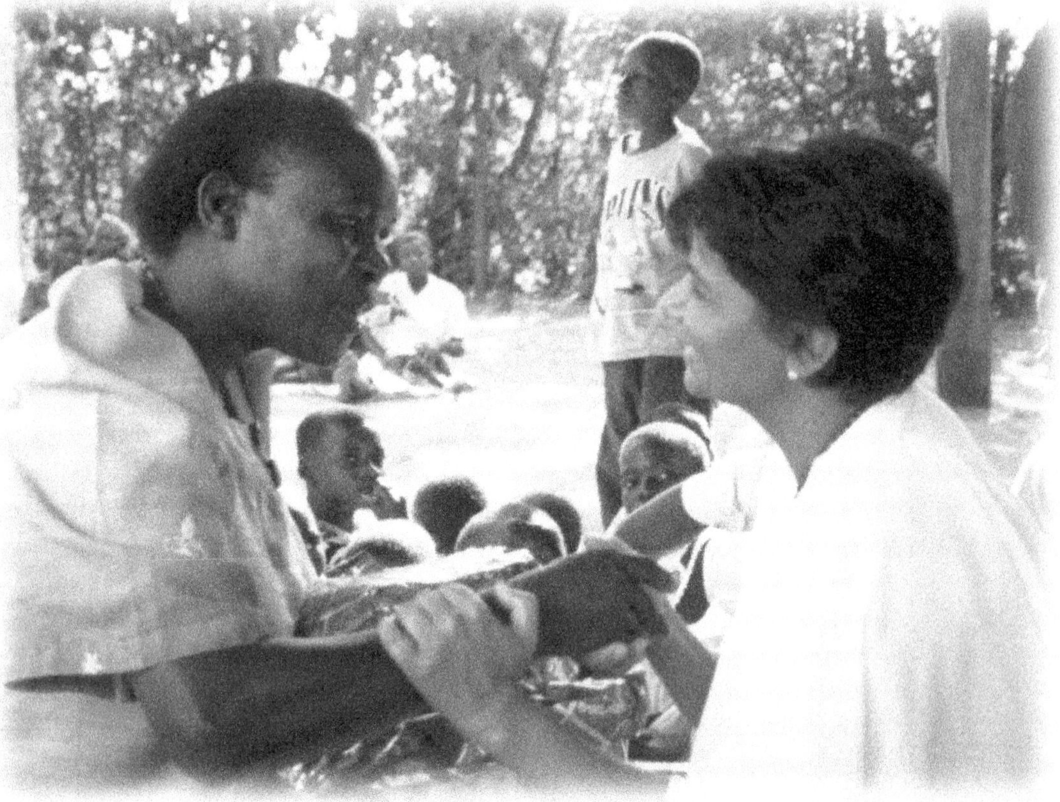

Sai Maa greets a Ugandan woman while serving villages and orphanages impacted by HIV/AIDS.

19

Integrating Divine Consciousness

Allow the Light that you are to shine,

to emanate from you, so that everywhere you are,

this Light will become activated.

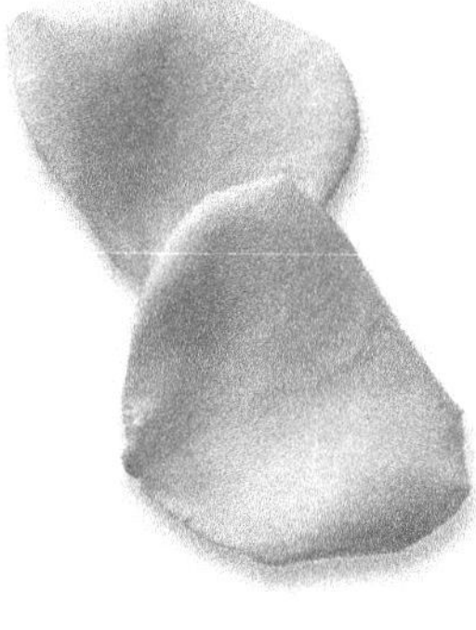

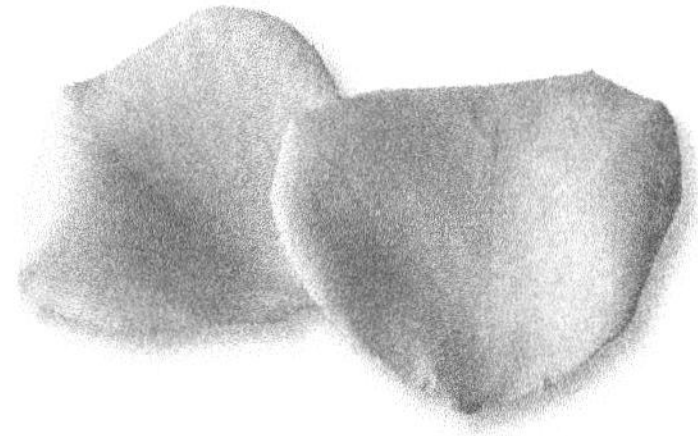

Integrating Divine Consciousness

Grace Waits for Your Permission

In each of you I welcome the Mother; in each of you I welcome the Father, in each of you, the Christ. We are numerous, very numerous, supporting you in your choice, your desire, to evolve to a truer humanity, to your own state of mastery, to coevolve together. What a joy it is to see a circle of Light created, integrating your Light with your physicality. What a joy to see you go beyond your physical consciousness, to perceive, to feel, and to *be* this consciousness that you are, vast, pure, luminous, and unlimited.

You were divine consciousness before being a human being. Now, create your existence on earth with the collaboration of the Creator. There is joy in seeing you accept your essence, accept your birthright, which is beyond the word "joy."

Manifest your great and perfectly divine Self. Your I AM has great beauty. Infinite power belongs to you, but be careful and use this for everyone and not only for your own needs. Advance toward this Light that belongs to you, without fear of advancing. You incarnated to manifest this Light and to serve others to find the path of serenity. Ask and you will receive. This Grace waits for your permission.

Through your Love, through your non-judgment, all of your thought forms can change. Transformation is within everyone's reach. It is only a question of choice—remember Jesus, Buddha, Mary Magdalene, and others. All of us must lead Mother Earth toward a higher consciousness, so let us choose peace, harmony, joy, and Love. Let us consciously choose.

When you are dropping the small personality, the small self, stay centered on the Impersonal Self, the Universal Self, and do not give importance to the hazards, the negativities. Show the ego that you are the master. When we work toward a goal, we center ourselves on the goal and not on the small difficulties we encounter as we work toward that goal. Do the same. As you know, rosebushes have thorns, but you also know that close to the rose there are no thorns; therefore, focus and center on the rose and not on the thorns.

Together you can gather your Love, your power, and serve the Light. The Light will filter little by little into this world. Meet together often and form circles of Light. The cosmos has equipped you with phenomenal potential. Use it. Universal joy and universal abundance belong to you. Give and you will receive a hundredfold.

Let us go forward together, having no fear of advancing, daring to unite without fear, not fearing to go too fast. Heavenly energy goes faster than the speed of Light. Do you believe that God is slower? You are all participating in the magnificent evolutionary plan of humanity. You can truly feel within yourself your life's choice.

Help humanity to wake up because you incarnated as a master for this reason. Courage, will, and truth are ready to serve you. Integrate this Christ Consciousness and live this supreme vision of Love. The heavenly worlds await your decisions in order to serve you. Let us be the carriers of this supreme Light.

Let us dare! Doubts will arise, but go beyond them. As you are being purified by the Light, these doubts will manifest.

The path of awakening belongs to you, so live simply, without artifice, without attachments. Attachments will sow fears, feelings of need, but know that God is in you, with you, around you, and *is* you. So what can you lack? Some settle into their little comforts with the false belief that they are secure. But you must live in equilibrium and in harmony. Join with the Light, and you will pass through the turbulence of this life without malaise.

It is very important to find this equilibrium of the body, the soul, and the spirit (the mental). With Grace, allow your faith to grow and reclaim your birthright. Reclaim it and your *faith will manifest that birthright.*

Fall asleep in this sublime Light and wake up having this Light as your first thought. All of your conscious hours will be luminous, will be in joy and Love, be in the glory of Christ and in harmony. This is the Light, free to express itself. Do not fear, you have much support. Give yourself to your Self. This truth does not change; it never changes.

This is truly a fabulous time to be on this planet. In Unity with all, you will succeed—in other words, succeed in Unity. This is no longer the time to isolate yourself, but to open yourself and go beyond your fears, to live your everyday life with spirituality. Those who resist will be there to prevent you from being who you are, but go beyond! Go beyond the borders of the belief systems of heaven and hell. Live from inside! Do not let yourself be trapped by the "mental" or by those who are afraid of going too far. Live in the serenity that you are not alone and advance with determination. Divine consciousness can do you no harm.

God, your Creator, loves you beyond what your intellect can grasp. You are the transmitters, the vectors, of this divine Love, of these celestial energies. The Love, Grace, happiness, and joy of this Christ energy cannot be described with words. The energy of Christ is purity. Here is the evolution of humanity into *divine* humanity.

Allow the Light that you are to shine, to emanate from you, so that everywhere you are, this Light will become activated. For eons you have lived in falseness, in untruth. Are you ready to change your attitude? Are you ready to no longer feed and nourish that which is false, that which creates fear? Are you ready to stop giving free expression to your senses? Are you ready to not be your "moods" but, on the contrary, to master them? What are you ready to do, ready to *be*?

Remember that knowledge and wisdom are in each cell of your being—yes, each *cell of your being*. You are energy. You are Light. Just because you have taken a physical body does not mean that you are no longer energy, that you are no longer Light. You carry divine consciousness within *you*.

During these changes there are moments of purification. Maybe you are eating more or less, sleeping more or less, in solitude, in withdrawal, laughing, giving yourself to others, overflowing with energy. A lot of things are happening; this is a birth and you are birthing yourself. There are two births: one physical and one spiritual. Do not allow yourself to be stuck in the malaise of this third dimension. It is not worth it. You have experienced it many times. Be free again, as when you were a Light body, but this time the Light body will be integrated into the physical body. Live in the third dimension on *this* plane.

Realize Your Divine Consciousness

Work with the Shakti of the cosmos, the creation of the cosmos, pure consciousness manifesting into the other pole, matter, or matrix. This very plunge of consciousness into matter starts the process of creation, our galaxy system, prebiological matter, biological, and primitive life forms, ascending through the chain to a certain perfection.

The next evolutionary step is to realize that you are divine. That Divinity is beginning to dawn, and the destiny of humanity is to culminate in divine consciousness. At this time, you are to be divine, to be Godly, to be Supra-conscious Beings. Free will is the key to your evolution, because free will or the freedom to evolve is inherent in each of you.

The human race will eventually experience enlightenment, but when will it happen? *When* depends on each individual. The more you are aligned with your true Self, the more Unity and Love will exist on Earth. Whatever is in disunity is a result of fear, a result of being afraid of the infinite power within. Live with the will to come to terms with this fear, to face these "obstacles" and to move on, to be honest with yourself. Only then is truth manifested.

Now is the time. This human race is at a grand crossroads, stepping onto the great spiral path of enlightenment, into the bright, golden destiny that is waiting as the reward. This is a golden opportunity to realize your fullness, your glorious potential, to use divine, advanced knowledge to solve so many environmental, social, and medical issues. The collective willingness allows the masses to move to a higher level of consciousness much faster than you would imagine.

Major shifts are happening. So many of you ask how many steps there are to reach the goal. Well, the first step, your first intention, is of great importance. Let's start together, heart in heart, hand in hand, so victory will be manifested. Just allow yourself to be led by the Light, and do not fear. You are supported. Let the Light shine through you, then the Love *is*. Thus you are living in peace.

The circle is completed with you, by you, and through you. All of humanity is going through a transitional phase, and this is just the beginning of the shift. Many are going to evolve faster, and they will assist others to speed up. In that shift, the mind will be more of a divine mind, goodness will be obvious, matter will be more refined, and matter will also be so alive, expressing itself in a divine way.

The energy grids around this planet are also undergoing major shifts, pulling the planetary energies into a new alignment. Through this process a new sphere of energy will be available, which will make the work for all much easier when they attune themselves to this new vibration. Thus they will accelerate this evolutionary process.

Move, move beyond the five senses. Higher vibration is here for you for the great union, which is impossible to be felt by the five senses. Your karma will be washed at great speed. Whatever you will feel will be due to your past feelings, actions, and thoughts.

Start to align your energy, your frequency, with beings of Light. With the sixth sense, attuning yourself to different kinds of energies, different levels of vibrations will be experienced naturally. Evolved humans will no longer be sick, and dis-ease will disappear. Harmony awaits the human race. What a grand journey to enjoy, and for that to happen you are to live a spiritual existence.

All can happen. It's a matter of choice, of willingness—and it will happen only if humans *choose*. Confront your challenges with Divinity and move from the fifth sense to the sixth sense. The movement, the wave, has already begun through your gaze inward. It's all there.

Immense choices await you. Human beings are capable of consciously cooperating with the power of evolution. Evolution no longer needs to be blind or instinctive. Only you can speed up and perfect what the "future" is to be. The work of bringing the matter into Light, raising the level of consciousness, is the only means for you to move from a depressed, lost and disoriented state to a much clearer state, ultimately to a breakthrough into higher consciousness. For inner development you must be aware that the physical, psychological, emotional, mental, and subtle dimensions are to be transformed through the work of Love, wisdom, power, knowledge, and spiritual practice.

So surrender, trust, and have faith in your inner Shakti, the Supreme Intelligence. Absorb the Light as much as possible and be with the Light and its power. Raise yourself into higher levels of consciousness and divinize this earthly consciousness, your personality, your mind, karma, and matter.

Your matter, therefore, must change. The only way for that to happen is to bring more and more Light into it, into its texture. Then it will be so alive it will go beyond death or dis-ease. Bring down the sacred fire, the fire of life, into the matter, and live freely on this plane with no more fear of death. Then this will be heaven on Earth, a new Earth.

Sai Maa blessing a pundit (Vedic priest) at the Satuwa Baba Ashram in Varanasi, India.

20

The Divine Work

You are to do the work to bring down this Light,

and for that you are to be devoted to the Light.

You are to devote yourself to that

with unwavering centeredness.

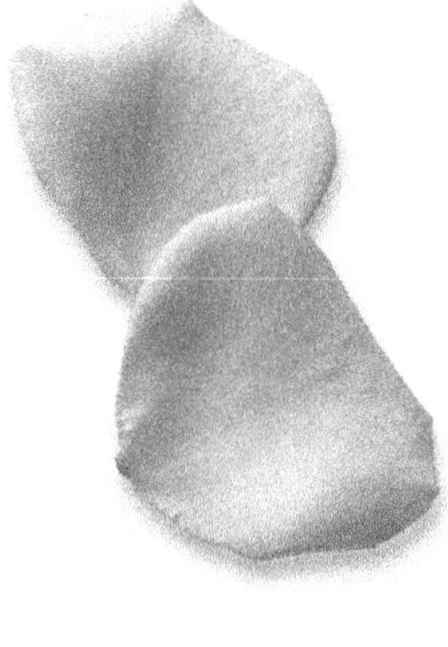

The Divine Work

Reestablish Your True Priorities

Embodiments of Love, is there any truth in this world? Is there any greatness in this world? If there is any for me, where is it in this world of duality? For me it lies within the human heart. It lies within the human being. Whenever the Self, the Christ, the Godhead, the Universe, or Allah reveals itself, it always occurs in a human being through the gateway of the heart.

Through Love—only through Love—the Self reveals itself, the Beloved reveals itself. Only Love will attract God or the Self so that this revelation is made manifest. And you are That, you are that Grace.

The work, then, is to move from the limited concept of identity caused by fear to identification with the Divine within. Overcome fear that leads to attachment, attachments such as personal belongings, the body, relationships, and so forth. Humans are always in fear, fear of losing. This is because of identification with the body, with body-consciousness and with the physical body, instead of identifying with the Eternal Self, with the One who is breathing within.

In this way, you are to use this birth to know yourself, to experience your own inner consciousness, and to find out who you truly are; otherwise, this is a waste. It is a waste if you live unconsciously. Oh, Dearest Ones, Embodiments of Love, there is this benevolent force behind all Creation—waves of Love, of Light sustained by truth. And you are that truth. That is your essence. That force is a Love that cannot be comprehended with the human mind; it is all-knowing, all-powerful, and all-compassionate. Compassion is that Love with understanding, where there is no judgment. It is all bliss, all Higher Self, all changeless and eternal truth.

Naturally, this law of consciousness, consciousness of Unity, is constantly breathing inside each of you. This natural law of consciousness is God breathing in and out, So Ham breathing in and out, inside you. God and soul are united in a physical body. Isn't that the amazing Grace of cosmic law? You are receiving an opportunity to experience that Grace, that law. This is freedom. *This is freedom.* Be free from this duality, from this suffering.

A human birth is so precious. A human being is sublime, so noble and great and very high. Of all creatures, the human being is the grandest, the highest. A human life is precious. It is very important to understand that a human is to experience this life, this *gift* of life, this miracle of life, in a worthy way.

Be aware, therefore, of this wondrous potential within. Feel your breath. Who is breathing? The power of the life force is in the breath, this breath of life. The vastness of divine Love is in the breath. The Light is in the breath, and the fullness of divine power is also in the breath. Truth is in that breath.

The whole universe is created out of that Grace of truth, out of that Grace of Love, from this power of the "one breath." And this "one breath" is between the inhale and the exhale. This "one breath" is so subtle that there is no breath. It is *fully* empty. This emptiness, this glory, this victory, is there, the eternal breath of the One.

So again and again I tell you, My Beloveds, awareness is crucial in your sadhana, crucial in this moment of great transformation on this exquisite planet where we are meeting. Our togetherness is in this exquisite place, and to you who read these words, I offer my humble gratitude. My vision is that you "come alive," be enlivened. That can happen as soon as you live in the awareness of your inner consciousness or Higher Self. Then you can only experience Love, joy, peace, harmony, and vastness. And when you walk, you will be that heaven on earth, and you will spread that Love. First, Love is inside you, within your Self, then it emanates, it radiates out of you and spreads around you.

Keep in mind that each of you on this plane *creates* your own heaven or hell—you create it *within*. No one creates it for you, so be aware of the Presence that offers this awareness, awareness of centeredness, of the golden Light of your inner Christ, the supreme power of the present, the inner silence. You are to experience that inner silence. Resting in that stillness, divine Presence resides inside you. Reestablish your resolution to live and experience that Presence fully.

Reestablish your true priorities. What is your choice in this life experience? Is it to push this Presence away and welcome every other thing that dishonors you, that dis-empowers you? Are you choosing to welcome this Divinity, this God, this Christ, and be free, be whole and Holy? Or are you choosing to be distracted?

Are you willing to live your purpose? All of you took birth for a purpose. Are you willing to experience the reason you came here, ready to live in union with your potential, your inner Shakti? Are you ready to honor humanity, ready to honor yourself? What is the teaching of Jesus? In your culture you cannot miss his incarnation, whether or not you trust that teaching. He is a great siddha, a great embodiment of Love. Are you ready to embody his teaching, ready to serve the highest, the grandest, with Love?

Only when you love humanity are you serving God, loving God, and honoring God—this is puja. But serving God is not doing years of japa, doing puja in your room and then being dry towards humanity. This is not the goal of worship. All of the great teaching asks you to embody the Self that you are, to embody the consciousness that you are. Listen to the words of the great masters and practice them. This is life. This is puja. This is worship. You are here to restore the original design of heaven on earth. In other words, you were created to divinize humanity, starting with yourself, a humanity full of heart.

The Celestial Realms Are Here, Now

Embodiments of Light, the original divine "blueprint" is ready to be activated, and in that "blueprint" is the Presence. Encoded in your DNA is the eternal truth, the "one breath" of perfect union, the breath of Oneness. Through awareness and all together, we can love all and uplift the planetary consciousness by being peace itself, by bringing the Light of the I AM Presence, the Paramatman, here for all.

This transformation in your heart, this freedom in your being, this liberation from maya, from duality, is realization, is moksha, and is realization of God within. This is the Grace of Self, and only that is permanent. Stay focused. Walk in that Grace, live in that Grace, and trust that teaching. Live with a mantle of divine Love. All of you are connected with great teaching, so honor that teaching.

Fulfill your dharma now. Do not waste a second. Do not wait. The celestial realms are here for you. They are not waiting until the last moment when you leave the planet for you to experience this Light and find this realm. You have this precious birth, and why do you celebrate your birthday? If it's precious, use it and perform good actions so you will realize you are this Light being. And think good thoughts so you "all ways" feel uplifted.

Uplift others with your Shakti, even in silence. All those around you will experience your Light and feel your enthusiasm and passion, your dedication and willingness. They will experience the Grace of your inner Self—your honoring the Higher Self in each being. See everyone as a being of Light, welcome them into your heart with Love, and accept them with gratitude. Recognize and treat all beings with respect, and you will honor the Self that is in you *and* in them, allowing the gateway to your sacred heart to open.

For that you are to be pure and to think pure thoughts. You are to live humbly, to be humble. Humility and devotion are the main attributes that will attract you to the Grace of the great teaching. That teaching is the power of the I AM Presence, the Light of the Paramatman, and the magnificence and glory of the Christ within the Higher Self.

Only when these attributes are active will the Highest start to embody the personality. If the personality is weak or emotional, the Presence will not be attracted to come closer. The Presence draws closer to a strong personality, so with your thoughts create a strong, pure personality. Your thoughts will create that strength because the Grace and blessings are "all ways" there for you.

Still, remember that you are to do the work. Do not just sit there and do nothing, and then move into pain, suffering, and emotional patterns. Do the work and practice the teaching. Practice the knowledge of these great masters. You are to work with unwavering focus for the descent of the Light, so do not allow yourself to be distracted by these worldly concerns which have absorbed you for so long. Find the mystery of the human being.

Do the work. Drop all fears, all attachments and desires. Drop even the desire for enlightenment, because that desire becomes an object. Be devoted because without devotion you will never experience moksha. Enlighten your personality with the divine attributes of Grace and with total faith. Only after you enlighten your personality can you choose to move into that truth, can you experience enlightenment. Then divine will, coupled with dedication to the Light, is so easily made manifest.

Welcome divine consciousness in your mind. Welcome the Divine in your consciousness and in your physicality. Embodiments of the Divine, remember to welcome God with devotion. Welcome God in all your actions and in all your thoughts. Magnify the Love in your heart. Your heart is "all ways" open. Never say your heart is closed, because it is not true. The heart will "all ways" be open, but your mind will veil the heart. So welcome purity in your mind. Magnify the Presence, the vibration, and the truth, and experience a life of Divinity.

Inhale the Presence at this moment. Inhale this truth. Inhale through all the petals of your chakras. Breathe and inhale this Presence with all your subtle bodies. Allow the Light, the Presence, the truth of all your chakras to expand in all the glands and organs of your body, your cells, molecules, and atoms.

Finally, live a noble life. Know that the Grace is right here with you and for you. Do not say you need Grace. You are to do the work to bring down this Light, and for that you are to be devoted to the Light. You are to devote yourself to that with unwavering centeredness. Invoke and call forth, bring forth with willingness. From deep within, activate the Christ Self and the Mother Divine.

Amid the distractions of the day, keep coming back to this present moment, this divine moment, this "now" moment in the sacred heart of the Beloved, the changeless within yourself, beyond space and time. How silent, how expanded is this "now." Beyond all thoughts and emotions, beyond body consciousness, move into this center of fullness, of nothingness, into the void. When all your attention goes only to this divine space, your whole being becomes divinized; then rest in it. Reside in that eternal moment of Grace created for you by your Self, by your Beloved and *with* your Beloved. Ask yourself, "Who inside is breathing? Who grants me the Grace of union?" It is the Beloved.

Your Beloved is God, is truth and Light, is the Self and the Christ, and is pure consciousness, different names for the One. There is nothing to lose. Fear not, My Dear Ones, do not fear, because there is nothing to lose in the reunion with your Beloved. You only can experience expansion and freedom. Freedom. The Grace of the perfect union waits for you.

Of course, you must be focused and be centered, because this is where freedom lies. Abide in the silence. In that space between two breaths, the One, the "now" is there. How *precious* is this present moment, this giving of the "now." Simply allow all to happen. Meditation is not just concentration; it is *deep* concentration. You are doing nothing. It is a tool that takes you to your being, *to your divine Presence.*

Go into that stillness. Go into that silence, the Eternal. Precious Ones, what about the unknown? Experience the unknown, the mystery, the infinite consciousness of Divinity—this is awareness. Be conscious. Be aware. You are forever free and infinite. Part of this consciousness has taken form as a body to experience itself, to experience separateness. The body has taken birth, but in truth you are birth-less and deathless. Life is a miracle.

Magnify your dedication. Magnify your devotion to the Light, *for* the Light, constantly. The Eternal Self, this ever-flowing consciousness, resides here at this moment, in you, *as* you, waiting for your permission to be revealed to you. The grandeur of the Supreme Self is in your heart.

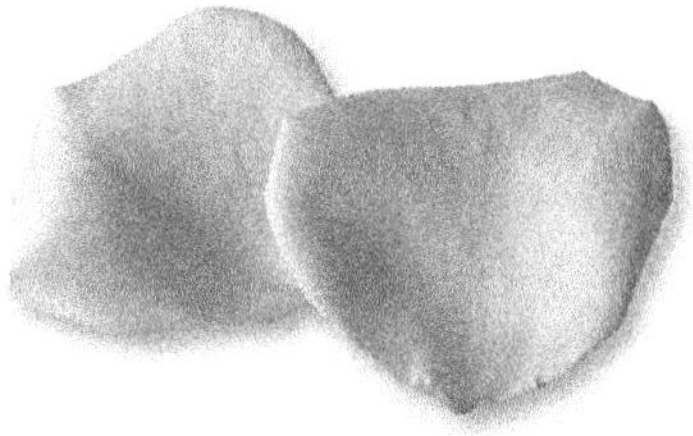

About the Author

Sai Maa is a world-renowned spiritual master, healer, and humanitarian. With a unique fusion of Eastern spiritual wisdom, Western therapeutic knowledge, and energetic mastery, Sai Maa shares teachings to uplift and empower others to master their lives as she has her own. Teaching from personal life experience, Sai Maa guides people in awakening and living from the highest potential inherent within them. Through all of her work, Sai Maa shares a rare depth of unconditional love and passion for life that manifests in the compassion and commitment with which she approaches her mission of global enlightenment.

Sai Maa was born on the island of Mauritius, a country known for embracing all religions and spiritual traditions. This spirit of openness, acceptance, and interfaith cooperation, helped shape Sai Maa's universal message of unity and compassion. At an early age Sai Maa demonstrated esoteric healing powers, which blossomed as her mission unfolded.

At the age of 21 Sai Maa moved to France, soon thereafter married a research scientist, and became the mother of two children. Sai Maa created a thriving therapy practice by merging her energetic healing powers with Western therapeutic training. She became certified in naturopathic, homeopathic, and osteopathic therapies. Also active in politics, Sai Maa served for years on the

Bordeaux City Council, helping to reform health care in the European Union on behalf of the French government. During this period, she met and became a life-long devoted disciple of the highly revered spiritual leader and world teacher, Sathya Sai Baba; as well as an active supporter of his humanitarian work.

Even with a successful career and rich family life Sai Maa knew, by the grace of her guru and through dedicated spiritual practice, that she had a greater life purpose. When her children were teenagers, she made the decision to step beyond traditional family roles, career, and politics, to dedicate her life to uplifting humanity by serving its conscious evolution.

Sai Maa has always made it clear that she does not want to cultivate followers; rather, she wishes to create masters who are capable of transforming the planet as embodiments of love and light. She tours the world, and educates thousands on a wide range of spiritual, social, and psychological topics, through transformative workshops, conference calls, writings, recordings, online programs, tools and technologies. Sai Maa has created many powerful practices including Sai Maa Diksha (the transmission of light into the brain of others and oneself, initiating the process of enlightenment), and Brain Illumination Meditation (a self-guided transformation through the use of light).

Sai Maa founded Humanity In Unity, a non-profit organization in the US, and the Sai Maa Vishnu Shakti Trust, a registered Indian charity, to support her humanitarian work. That work includes projects to provide food, clothing, clean water, and medical care, to children and families and to support widows and orphans. Sai Maa's global community is represented by various centers and groups around the world. Members gather to support spiritual practice and humanitarian activities.

In 2007 Sai Maa was honored with the prestigious title of Jagadguru, the highest title in the Vedic tradition of India. She is the first woman to receive this title in the 2,700 years of the Vishnuswami lineage. The title was given to Sai Maa in recognition of her humanitarian service and her spiritual mastery. This honor represents one among many, all of which recognize the depth of Sai Maa's wisdom and contribution to the evolution of humanity and the planet.

Sai Maa in Allahabad, India, receiving initiation as a Jagadguru, the highest title in the Vedic tradition of India.

Notes

One: *Be the Embodiment of Love*

1. **The practice of japa.** "The japa is usually successful only on one of two conditions—if it is repeated with a sense of its significance, a dwelling of something in the mind on the nature, power, beauty, attraction of the Godhead it signifies and is to bring into the consciousness,—that is the mental way; or if it comes up from the heart or rings in it with a certain sense or feeling of bhakti making it alive,—that is the emotional way. Either the mind or the vital has to give it support or sustenance." For more, see Sri Aurobindo, *The Integral Yoga* (Pondicherry, India: Sri Aurobindo Ashram Trust, 1993) 166.

2. **Shakti.** "In the world so far as man is concerned we are aware only of mind-energy, life-energy, energy in Matter; but it is supposed that there is a spiritual energy or force also behind them from which they originate. All things, in either case, are the results of a Shakti, energy or force." See Sri Aurobindo, *Letters on Yoga*, vol. I (Pondicherry, India: Sri Aurobindo Ashram Trust, 1970) 216.

Two: *The Grace Latent in All*

1. **The I AM.** "The failure of outer things to satisfy, leads the soul to seek the power within. Then the individual may discover that I AM, he may know that within him lies all power to satisfy the soul, to fulfill its every need and desire. This knowledge may not come until the individual is driven by the buffetings of the world to seek this inner plane of peace and calm. When he knows I AM is the fulfillment of his desire, the desire is filled." See Baird Spalding, *Life and Teaching of the Masters of the Far East*, vol. 1 (Marina Del Rey, CA.: DeVorss & Co., 1935) 143.

Three: *The Source of Joy and Bliss*

1. **Welcoming joy.** "Meanwhile peace and joy can be there permanently, but the condition of this permanence is that one should have the constant contact or indwelling of the Divine, and this comes naturally not to the outer mind or vital but to the inner soul or psychic being. Therefore one who wants his yoga to be a path of peace or joy

must be prepared to dwell in his soul rather than in his outer mental and emotional nature." See Sri Aurobindo, *Letters on Yoga*, vol. III (Pondicherry, India: Sri Aurobindo Ashram Press, 1970) 1320.

Four: *The Truth of Relationships*

1. **The role of the Supreme Self in your relationship.** "In any case human affection whatever its value has its place, because through it the psychic being gets the emotional experiences it needs until it is ready to prefer the true to the apparent, the perfect to the imperfect, the divine to the human. As the consciousness has to rise to the higher level so the activities of the heart also have to rise to that higher level and change their basis and character. Yoga is the founding of all life and consciousness in the Divine, so also love and affection must be rooted in the Divine and a spiritual and psychic oneness in the Divine must be their foundation—to reach the Divine first leaving other things aside or to seek the Divine alone is the straight road towards that change. That means no attachment—it need not mean turning affection into disaffection or chill indifference." See Aurobindo, *The Integral Yoga* 326-27.

Five: *Forgiveness Brings Freedom*

1. **Moksha (liberation).** "A deep, intense or massive substance of peace and stillness is very commonly the first of its powers that descends and many experience it in that way. At first it comes and stays only during meditation or, without the sense of physical inertness or immobility, a little while longer and afterwards is lost; but if the sadhana follows its normal course, it comes more and more, lasting longer and in the end as an enduring deep peace and inner stillness and release becomes a normal character of the consciousness, the foundation indeed of a new consciousness, calm and liberated." See Aurobindo, *Letters*, vol. III, 1197.

2. **Samskaras.** "In the subconscient [sic] there is an obscure mind full of obstinate Sanskaras [sic], impressions, associations, fixed notions, habitual reactions formed by our past, an obscure vital full of the seeds of habitual desires, sensations and nervous reactions, a most obscure material which governs much that has to do with the condition of the body. It is largely responsible for our illnesses; chronic or repeated illnesses are indeed mainly due to the subconscient and its obstinate memory and habit of repetition of whatever has impressed itself upon the body-consciousness." See Aurobindo, *Letters*, vol. I, 353.

3. **Our subtle bodies.** "There are different names for these subtle bodies. The names that I use are, from the inside out, the etheric body, the emotional body, the mental body and the next layer out is what I call the causal body. Most people, including clairvoyants, aren't perceiving beyond the causal body in one lifetime. Many times when people think they are, they are really perceiving different levels or layers *within* the causal body. You see, each subtle body has different frequency subdivisions within it. The causal body is more spiritual than the first three subtle bodies (the etheric, emotional and mental) but less purely spiritual compared to the ones which come after it. The causal body is key because it's a bridge between the lower bodies and the higher bodies that come after it." For more, see Virginia Essene and Irving Feurst, eds., *Energy Blessings from the Stars* (Santa Clara, Ca.: Spiritual Education Endeavors Publishing Co., 1998) 23.

Six: *The Nature of the Mind*

1. **Tapping into the present and the Presence.** "As you become more conscious of your present reality, you may suddenly get certain insights as to *why* your conditioning functions in those particular ways; for example, why your relationships follow certain patterns, and you may remember things that happened in the past or see them more clearly. That is fine and can be helpful, but it is not essential. What is essential is your conscious presence. *That* dissolves the past. That is the transformative agent. So, don't seek to understand the past, but be as present as you can. The past cannot survive in your presence. It can only survive in your absence." See Eckhart Tolle, *The Power of Now* (Novato, CA.: New World Library, 1997) 78.

2. **Using the mantra.** "During periods of doubt, anxiety, or dispersion, the repetition of the mantra soothes and collects one's consciousness.

"To be effective the mantras should be done without desire for personal benefit. This helps to bring about an attitude of inner detachment, wherein one's inner self can be experienced. For this reason, they frequently end with the word 'Namaha', meaning 'to surrender' or 'salutation' to the Divine." For further study, see M. Govindan, *Babaji and the 18 Siddha Kriya Yoga Tradition* (St. Etienne de Bolton, Quebec: Kriya Yoga Publications, 1991) 174.

Seven: *The Transformative Power of Meditation*

1. **Bhakti.** "The nature of bhakti is adoration, worship, self-offering to what is greater than oneself; the nature of love is a feeling or a seeking for closeness and union.

Self-giving is the character of both; both are necessary in the yoga and each gets its full force when supported by the other." For more detail, see Aurobindo, *Integral Yoga* 159.

2. **So Ham.** "When the students realize, through deep meditation and absolute Truth, they reply only 'Su–ham.' The teacher says to the student, 'Thou are God,' and the students reply, 'That I am, su-ham.' [sic]

"Let us look closer into the statement and the answers which the student gives when he realizes his Godhead, 'su-ham.' It contains two consonants and three vowels; the two consonants *s* and *h*, the three vowels *a*, *u*, and *m* which is a medial syllabic.

"The consonants cannot be pronounced unless joined to vowels. Thus in the domain of sound, the consonants represent the perishable, the vowels the imperishable.

"Therefore *s* and *h* are relegated to the perishable. A-U-M remains, and form AUM the eternal." See Baird Spalding, *Life and Teaching of the Masters of the Far East*, vol. III (Marina Del Rey, CA.: DeVorss & Co., 1935) 126.

Eight: *Awaken to the Truth of Your Being*

1. **I AM That I AM.** "And Moses said unto God, Behold, when I come unto the children of Israel, and shall say unto them, The God of your fathers hath sent me unto you; and they shall say to me, What is his name? What shall I say unto them?

"And God said unto Moses, I AM THAT I AM: and he said, Thus shalt thou say unto the children of Israel, I AM hath sent me unto you." Exodus 3: 13, 14 (King James Bible).

2. **Mother Kundalini Shakti.** "It is here coiled up and asleep in all the centres of our inner being (Chakras) and is at the base what is called in the Tantras the Kundalini Shakti. But it is also above us, above our head as the Divine Force—not there coiled up, involved, asleep, but awake, scient [sic], potent, extended and wide; it is there waiting for manifestation and to this Force we have to open ourselves—to the power of the Mother." For further study see Aurobindo, *Integral Yoga* 221.

Nine: *Sadhana, the Path to Grace*

1. **Maintaining vigilance.** "For when the condition is good, the lower movements have a habit of subsiding and become quiescent, hiding as it were,—or they go out of the nature and remain at a distance. But if they see that the sadhak is losing vigilance, then they slowly begin to rise or draw near, most often unseen, and when he is quite off his guard, surge up suddenly or make a sudden irruption. This continues until the

whole nature, mental, vital, physical down to the very subsconscient [sic] is enlightened, conscious, full of the Divine. Till that happens, one must always remain watchful in a sleepless vigilance." See Aurobindo, *Letters*, vol. III 1711.

Ten: *The Sadhaka's Prayer*

1. **Using the Sadhaka's Prayer.** "Repeating this to yourself or aloud is the opportunity to call upon your I Am Presence, your Supreme Self, all those Divine Beings and the Elohim of the Violet Ray. Always here to serve you, they assist you to live divinely at this moment in your daily life, to create divinely, to manifest perfection with every thought, word, and action. You can also add to this Prayer whatever you choose to ask for and you will receive assistance." Swami Parameshwarananda (Paul Faerstein), e-mail to the editor, 21 Feb. 2005.

Eleven: *Align with Your Supreme Self*

1. **Saying "yes" to the Light.** "The Light is the light of the Divine Consciousness. The aim of this yoga is first to come into contact with this consciousness and then to live in its light and allow the light to transform the whole nature, so that the being may live in union with the Divine and the nature become a field for the action of the divine Knowledge, the divine Power and the divine Ananda." See Aurobindo, *Letters On Yoga*, vol. II (Pondicherry, India: Sri Aurobindo Ashram Press, 1970) 550-51.

2. **The precious "now."** "Why is it the most precious thing? Firstly, because it is the only thing. It's all there is. The eternal present is the space within which your whole life unfolds, the one factor that remains constant. Life is now. There was never a time when your life was not now, nor will there ever be.

"Secondly, the Now is the only point that can take you beyond the limited confines of the mind. It is your only point of access into the timeless and formless realm of Being." See Eckhart Tolle, *Practicing the Power of Now* (Novato, CA.: New World Library, 1997) 31.

Twelve: *Seek the Clarity of Higher Consciousness*

1. **Chakras.** "In the body (rather the subtle body than the physical, but connected with the corresponding parts in the gross physical body also) there are centres [chakras] proper to each level of the being. There is a centre at the top of the head and above it which is that of the above-mind or higher consciousness; a centre in the forehead between the eyebrows which is that of the thinking mind, mental will, mental vision; a centre in

the throat which is that of the expressive or externalizing mind: these are the mental centres. Below comes the vital—the heart (emotional), the navel (the dynamic life-centre), another below the navel in the abdomen which is the lower or sensational vital centre. Finally, at the bottom of the spine is the Muladhara or physical centre." See Aurobindo, *Letters*, vol. III 1142.

Thirteen: *What Is Your Choice?*

1. **Karma.** "At present we fix too much on the particular will and act of the moment and a particular consequence in a given time. But the particular only receives its value by all of which it is a part, all from which it comes, all to which it moves. We fix too much also on the externalities of karma and consequence, this good or that bad action and result of action. But the real consequence which the soul is after is a growth in the manifestation of its being, an enlarging of its range and action of power, its comprehension of delight of being, its delight of creation and self-creation, and not only its own but the same things in others with which its greater becoming and joy are one." See Sri Aurobindo, *Rebirth and Karma* (Wilmot, WI.: Lotus Light Publications, 1991) 90-91.

Fourteen: *The Eternal Nature of the Self*

1. **The consciousness waiting to be discovered.** "It is only if there is a greater consciousness beyond Mind and that consciousness is accessible to us that we can know and enter into the ultimate Reality. Intellectual speculation, logical reasoning as to whether there is or is not such a greater consciousness cannot carry us very far. What we need is a way to get the experience of it, to reach it, enter into it, live in it. If we can get that, intellectual speculation and reasoning must fall necessarily into a very secondary place and even lose their reason for existence." See Aurobindo, *Letters*, vol. I 158.

2. **Illness.** "It is like a wrong suggestion in the mind,—if the mind accepts it, it becomes clouded and confused and has to struggle back into harmony and clearness. It is so with the body consciousness and illness. You must not accept but reject it with your physical mind and so help the body consciousness to throw off the suggestion. If necessary, make a counter-suggestion 'No, I shall be well; I am and shall be all right.' And in any case call in the Mother's Force to throw out the suggestion and the illness it is bringing." For more on this subject, see Aurobindo, *Integral Yoga* 321.

Fifteen: *What Is Enlightenment?*

1. **The One—one Self.** "Humanity is more than a brotherhood. It is One Man, just as a vine and its branches is one vine. No one part or one unit can be separated from the whole. The Christ's prayer is "That they all may be One."" See Baird Spalding, *Life and Teaching of the Masters of the Far East*, vol. II (Marina Del Rey, CA.: DeVorss & Co., Publishers, 1972) 47.

Sixteen: *When You Surrender to God*

1. **Surrender.** "Self-giving or surrender is demanded of those who practice this Yoga, because without such a progressive surrender of the being it is quite impossible to get anywhere near the goal. To keep open means to call in her Force to work in you, and if you do not surrender to it, it amounts to not allowing the Force to work in you at all or else only on condition that it will work in the way you want and not in its own way which is the way of the Divine Truth." For more on surrender, see Aurobindo, *Integral Yoga* 100-101.

Seventeen: *The Glory of Seva*

1. **Knowing your supreme heart.** "Purifying the heart means after all a pretty considerable achievement and it is no use getting despondent, despairful, etc, because one finds things in oneself that still need to be changed. If one keeps the true will and true attitude, then the intuitions or intimations from within will begin to grow, become clear, precise, unmistakable and the strength to follow them will grow also: and then before even you are satisfied with yourself, the Divine will be satisfied with you and begin to withdraw the veil by which he protects himself and his seekers against a premature and perilous grasping of the greatest thing to which humanity can aspire." See Aurobindo, *Letters*, vol. II 904.

Eighteen: *Be Peace*

1. **Grace.** "It is not indispensable that the Grace should work in a way that the human mind can understand, it generally doesn't. It works in its own "mysterious" way. At first usually it works behind the veil, preparing things, not manifesting. Afterwards it may manifest, but the sadhak does not understand very well what is happening; finally, when he is capable of it, he both feels and understands or at least begins to do so. Some feel and understand from the first or very early; but that is not the ordinary case." See Aurobindo, *Letters*, vol. II 610-11.

Nineteen: *Integrating Divine Consciousness*

1. **Realizing you are Divine.** "I have learned that just as man may touch the earth with his feet, so on the wings of aspiration may he soar to celestial heights. Like those of old, he may walk the earth and talk with God; and the more he does so the more difficult it will be for him to discover where Universal Life ends and where individual existence begins. When man forms an alliance with God through spiritual understanding, the boundary line between God and man disappears. When this point is reached, man will know what Jesus meant when He said, 'I and my Father are one.'" See Spalding, *Life and Teaching*, vol. II 67.

Twenty: *The Divine Work*

1. **The "reunion" with your Beloved.** "From this Universal Consciousness, we can draw all knowledge; we know that we can know all, without studying and without process of reasoning, not going from one lesson to another nor from one point to another. The lessons are necessary only in order to bring us to the attitude in which we can step forth into this thought. Then we become comprehensive and include all thought. There is a complete stream of motivating thought that is irresistible and we know that nothing can divert us from true accomplishment. We are with the whole; thus we move on irresistibly with the whole. It is impossible for any condition to keep us from our accomplishment. The drop of water is only weak when it is removed from the ocean; replace it and it is as powerful as the whole ocean. It matters not whether we like it or whether we believe it. It is Intelligent Law and we are that very thing." See Spalding, *Life and Teaching*, vol. II 41-42.

Glossary

Akashic records
Compilation of energetic information which contains a record of every soul's past, present, and potential future thoughts, feelings, and actions.

Amrit or Amrita
Translates as immortality and is often used to denote the nectar of the Gods that bestows immortality. (Sanskrit)

Ananda
Spiritual bliss. (Sanskrit)

Ascended Master
One who was once a human being and has now achieved spiritual mastery through ascension of consciousness and matter. Ascended Masters are committed to serving and guiding the spiritual evolution of humankind from the higher dimensions of light.

Ascension
Transformation of matter into the higher frequencies of light and love. Ascension allows physical death to be bypassed through raising the vibration of the entire physical body into light.

Atma(n)
Self, Higher Self or Supreme Self. The true essence of the individual beyond body, mind, and emotions. (Sanskrit)

Baba
(See Sai Baba)

Bhakti
Devotion. Refers to the spiritual practice or the state of devotion leading to union with God (e.g., devotion to a spiritual teacher or guru). (Sanskrit)

Blue Pearl (also blue light)
Subtle energy structure located in the bindu (center of the crown chakra). It is considered the abode of the Supreme Self in the physical body. Most often seen with the inner eye during meditation.

Body Consciousness
State of consciousness or being associated with the physical body and physical plane.

Chakra
Spiritual energy vortices (centers) in the subtle body. There are seven major chakras in human beings, located from the base of the spine to the top of the head. (Sanskrit)

Chant (also bhajan)
Verbal repetition of sacred phrases or mantras, usually sung to music.

Christ Consciousness
State of consciousness in which one realizes union with the divine.

Christ Self
(see Higher Self)

Consciousness
Foundational state of beingness, the basic constituent of all existence.

Darshan
Vision or experience of the divine brought about by being in the presence of a holy person or sacred statue. (Sanskrit)

Deva(s)
Deity. Benevolent supernatural being. (Sanskrit)

Dharma
Concept of right action, duty, or destiny that is aligned with one's spiritual evolution. Natural laws of cosmic and social order. The law of righteousness. (Sanskrit)

Diksha
Initiation. Referring to a transference of divine energy from a master. Sai Maa Diksha is a powerful practice offered by Sai Maa for illuminating the brain. It is the physical transference of energy or divine light into the brain that initiates the process of enlightenment. (Sanskrit)

Divine Presence
(see I AM Presence)

Enlightenment
Spiritual liberation or Self-Realization. Being consciously and permanently awake in the I AM. A state of consciousness marked by the continuous presence of love, peace, and compassion, where a being permanently experiences the Higher Self as their true nature.

Grace
Divine gift and energy that allows all our spiritual efforts to be realized.

Guru
Translates as from darkness to light, and refers to a spiritual master who dedicates herself/himself to serving the transformation and evolution of others. (Sanskrit)

Higher Self (the Christ Self)
Dimension of our being that serves as a step-down transformer, regulating the amount and quality of energy that flows into the subtle and physical anatomy of the body from the higher dimension of the Presence. Our Higher Self holds the state of divine love and unity, and continually maintains a vision of the perfection that is the birthright of every human to manifest in the physical realm.

I AM Presence (also the I AM, the I AM Principle or the Presence)
The highest dimension of our being and represents the first projection of individuality from Source. The Presence is all the pure qualities of Source in its perfection. As we are the Presence in our essence, these pure qualities are our natural state of being.

Initiation
Ceremony by which the student is instructed in a spiritual practice by a spiritual teacher or guru; can also include an energetic transfer of energy to the student by the master.

Jai (also Jay or Jaya)
Translates as hail to or glory to. Usually used in a mantra, phrase, or chant that is praising an aspect of the divine. (Sanskrit)

Japa
Practice of rhythmic repetition of a sacred name or mantra. Japa is often practiced with a mala and is used to bring about a union of the mind with the divine. (Sanskrit)

Karma
Action. Referring to the universal principle of cause and effect. Karma is an energetic accumulation of all of the actions a given person has performed in their current and previous lives, and directly affects the experiences and circumstances that are drawn into that person's life. (Sanskrit)

Kundalini (also Mother Kundalini Shakti)
Powerful divine energy that lives within every human being in the base of the spine, most often in a dormant state. It is symbolized by a coiled snake whose awakening and movement through the chakras brings about great purification and inner bliss. (Sanskrit)

Maa (also Ma, Mata, Mataram, Mataji)
Mother or Divine Mother, used to show both affection and respect.

Maha Bhakti
Great love of and devotion to the divine. (Sanskrit)

Mala
String of 108 beads used in practicing japa. (Sanskrit)

Mandir
Sacred temple. (Sanskrit)

Mantra
Sacred word or phrase used in a prescribed way, often in repetition during meditation to focus the mind. (Sanskrit)

Maya
Translates as illusion or ignorance, and refers to that which veils the experience of the true reality of Unity. (Sanskrit)

Meditation
Type of spiritual practice used to focus the mind and develop an awareness of our divine nature. There are many forms of meditation that may include practices such as mantra, contemplation, conscious breathing, and visualization.

Moksha
Spiritual liberation, enlightenment. (Sanskrit)

Mother Kundalini Shakti
(see Kundalini)

Mother Divine
Feminine aspect of God.

Namaste
Greeting meaning I honor the divinity within you. Often spoken with palms together at the heart (as in prayer). (Sanskrit)

Om (also Aum)
Primordial sound by which the universe came into existence, holding within it the totality of creation. This sacred mantra is often chanted as a practice of aligning our energies with the divine impulse of creation.

Om Jai Jai Maa (also Om Jai Jai Sai Maa)
Mantra or greeting meaning Hail to Mother Divine or I honor the Divine Mother in you and in me. (Sanskrit)

Om Namah Shivaya
Mantra or greeting meaning I honor the divine within me or I honor Shiva (essence of pure space). (Sanskrit)

Paramatman
Supreme Self or Supreme Soul. (Sanskrit)

Permanent Atom
Focal point for the divine spark manifest within each one of us and carried from one incarnation to the next. Usually said to be located in the heart chakra or pineal gland.

Prana
Breath. Pure, life-giving force that resides within all. (Sanskrit)

Presence, the
(See I Am Presence)

Puja
Worship or ritual to invoke and give praise to an aspect of the divine represented in a picture, statue, sacred object or a living being. (Sanskrit).

Sacred Fire
Master power of life that resides within everyone and contains the power to manifest perfection in all.

Sadhana
Spiritual practice or discipline. The goal of sadhana is to attain spiritual realization. (Sanskrit)

Sadhaka
Spiritual aspirant, the practitioner of a spiritual discipline or sadhana. (Sanskrit)

Sadhu
One who takes an initiation of renunciation within the Vedic tradition in pursuit of spiritual attainment. (Sanskrit)

Sai Baba
Bhagavan Sri Sathya Sai Baba, affectionately called "Baba," is the Guru of Sai Maa. He is one of India's most revered spiritual masters and many consider him to be an Avatar (incarnation of God).

Samskara (or Sanskara)
Subtle energy impressions or imprints of past thoughts, feelings, and actions contained in the nervous system. (Sanskrit)

Sat-Chit-Ananda (also Sachchidananda)
Phrase meaning existence (Sat), consciousness (Chit), bliss (Ananda), referring to the sublimely blissful experience of divine consciousness. (Sanskrit)

Satsang
Translates as in the company of truth and refers to a gathering of spiritual seekers for the purpose of spiritual practice and study. (Sanskrit)

Self, the
(See Higher Self)

Seva
Selfless service. A spiritual practice of offering any form of service, simply for the sake of serving, without expectation of gain. (Sanskrit)

Shakti
Divine feminine creative power or energy that resides in all of life. The cosmic force of creation that is often represented as the Divine Mother. The transformative spiritual power radiated by a master or being of light. (Sanskrit)

Shiva
Divine presence or consciousness that destroys all ignorance and liberates the aspirant from the suffering of the changing, relative world. Pure space. (Sanskrit)

Siddha
One who has attained spiritual perfection through yoga. (Sanskrit)

So Ham (pronounced so hum)
Mantra meaning I AM and used as an affirmation of the divinity within. (Sanskrit)

Soul
In India, it is the Supreme Self, which is completely pure. In the West, it is considered the non-physical, spiritual accumulation of all one's lives.

Source
All-pervading Oneness from which all of creation arises, the All That Is.

Sri (or Shri)
Title of respect. (Sanskrit)

Subtle Bodies
Layers of subtle energy surrounding the physical body. Each band of frequencies has its own unique set of characteristics and together the subtle bodies are sometimes referred to as the aura.

Universal Consciousness
Eternal consciousness of the Higher Self. Realization of the eternal, indestructible, immortal nature of ourselves, beyond birth or death.

Vedas
Ancient sacred scriptures cognized by the seers of India and the basis of the Vedic tradition. They contain the wisdom of the universe and the nature of consciousness. (Sanskrit)

Yoga
Practice leading to the state of union with God, or that state of Oneness. (Sanskrit)